ACCLAIM FOR

King of Russia

"This is a fascinating look at how the current machine of Russian hockey runs, and provides much insight into how the NHL's importation of foreign players affects the leagues in their home countries."

– *Globe and Mail*

"I'm so impressed by this book that I'm almost overwhelmed.... It's an amazing look into just one year of an amazing life."

– Hockeybookreviews.com

"An entertaining story.... A colourful travelogue from St. Petersburg to Siberia, set against the contradictions of social change in Russia and a hockey league that is suddenly flush with petro-dollars."

– *Calgary Herald*

"Think of it as a cold, industrial, northern version of *A Year in Provence*. This is a place we might never wish to actually visit in the flesh, but in the reading it is absolutely enthralling."

– Roy MacGregor

"An insightful and entertaining read for hockey players and fans, but also for a travel buff or anyone interested in the changing society and economy of Russia."

– *London Free Press*

"Genuinely compelling.... If you're passionate about international hockey and want to understand why Russia keeps producing highly skilled players without winning the Olympics or Worlds, *King of Russia* is unquestionably the book to read this year."

– Hockeyadventure.com

МАГНИТОГОРСК
МЕТАЛЛУРГ
EASTO

KING OF RUSSIA
A YEAR IN THE RUSSIAN SUPER LEAGUE

DAVE KING with
ERIC DUHATSCHEK

EMBLEM
McClelland & Stewart

Cloth edition published 2007
Emblem edition published 2008

Emblem is an imprint of McClelland & Stewart Ltd.
Emblem and colophon are registered trademarks of McClelland & Stewart Ltd.

Library and Archives Canada Cataloguing in Publication

King, Dave (William David Brent), 1947–
King of Russia : a year in the Russian Super League /
Dave King ; with Eric Duhatschek.

ISBN 978-0-7710-9570-2

1. King, Dave (William David Brent), 1947–. 2. Metallurg Magnitogorsk (Hockey team). 3. Hockey – Russia (Federation). 4. Hockey coaches – Canada – Biography. 5. Hockey coaches – Russia (Federation) – Magnitogorsk – Biography. 6. Magnitogorsk (Russia) – Biography. I. Duhatschek, Eric, 1955– II. Title.

GV848.5.K56A3 2008 796.962092 C2008-900902-9

We acknowledge the financial support of the Government of Canada through the Book Publishing Industry Development Program and that of the Government of Ontario through the Ontario Media Development Corporation's Ontario Book Initiative. We further acknowledge the support of the Canada Council for the Arts and the Ontario Arts Council for our publishing program.

All photos in the text are courtesy of Dave and Linda King.

Typeset in Electra by M&S, Toronto
Printed and bound in Canada

McClelland & Stewart Ltd.
75 Sherbourne Street
Toronto, Ontario
M5A 2P9
www.mcclelland.com

1 2 3 4 5 12 11 10 09 08

To my darling wife, Linda, for her patience, her love, and her outstanding oatmeal chocolate chip cookies

DK

To Mary, Adam, and Paula, three good reasons to keep going when the going gets tough

ED

CONTENTS

Time out: Coaches Viktor Korolev, Dave King and Fedor Kanareykin talking to Evgeny Malkin, Evgeny Varlamov and Igor Korolev.

METALLURG MAGNITOGORSK
TEAM ROSTER 2005–06

MANAGEMENT

Viktor Rashnikov, *owner, oligarch, president of* MMK *Steel*
Gennady Velichkin, *general manager*
Oleg Kuprianov, *assistant general manager*
Dave King, *head coach*
Fedor Kanareykin, *assistant coach*
Viktor Korolev, *assistant coach*
Viktor Suchov, *assistant coach*
Yuri Shundrov, *assistant coach*
Viktor Gudzik, *fitness coach*
Igor Mouraviev, *translator*

PLAYERS

Travis Scott, *goaltender*
Konstantin Simchuk, *goaltender*
Anders Eriksson, *defence*
Vladislav Boulin, *defence*
Vitali Atyushov, *defence*
Evgeny Varlamov, *defence*
Alexander Boikov, *defence*
Alexander Seluyanov, *defence*
Vladimir Malenkikh, *defence*
Evgeny Biryukov, *defence*
Dmitri Yushkevich, *defence*
Evgeny Malkin, *forward*
Stanislav Chistov, *forward*
Igor Korolev, *forward*
Ilya Vorobiev, *forward*
Alexei Kaigorodov, *forward*
Alexei Tertyshny, *forward*
Dmitri Pestunov, *forward*
Nikolai Kulemin, *forward*
Eduard Kudermetov, *forward*
Ruslan Nurtdinov, *forward*
Evgeny Gladskikh, *forward*
Ravil Gusmanov, *forward*
Yuri Dobryshkin, *forward*
Denis Platonov, *forward*
Alexander Savchenkov, *forward*
Roman Kukhtinov, *defence*
Renat Ibragimov, *defence*

MMK steel factory as viewed from King's apartment window.

Magnitogorsk hockey arena as viewed from King's apartment window. The Ural river flows behind the arena.

PART I **SUMMER**

July 5, 2005

SOME PEOPLE TOLD ME I WAS CRAZY to do this, and at this precise moment I'm not sure I would disagree. I am standing on the ice surface at the Magnitogorsk Arena, in the heart of Mother Russia, my new home away from home for the next ten months. I am jet-lagged and sleep-deprived and fighting a lot of warring emotions. Thirty-six hours ago I was half a world away in Saskatoon, preparing for the adventure of a lifetime. Midway through last spring I'd been contacted by Serge Levin, a Russian hockey agent, to see if I was interested in becoming the first Canadian to coach a team in the Russian Super League. At the time, he didn't mention which team it might be. He only wanted to gauge my interest in coming to Russia in the first place.

During the past quarter of a century, the flow of hockey talent between Russia and North America has mostly gone in one direction. The NHL's appetite for more and better players saw them recruit heavily in Russia, and over time there have been Russians who've led the league in goal-scoring, Russians who've won the rookie of the year award, and dozens of Russians who've seen their names engraved on the Stanley Cup.

More recently, as a result of the political and economic upheaval that has characterized Russian life since the fall of Communism, there has been something of a reverse migration. Salaries have become more competitive there and a handful of teams, with dollars to burn, have lured some of their homegrown talent back.

Then, in the year of the NHL lockout, even some of our best-known Canadian players (Vincent Lecavalier, Dany Heatley, and Brad Richards, to name three) came to play in the Super League. But coaching? That was different. That had never been done before. There have been Russian assistant coaches in the NHL and a few European-born coaches in Russia, but no team had ever been willing to turn the keys over to a Canadian . . . until now.

Two days before I left Canada, I was in Eston, Saskatchewan, for a family get-together. And since training camps open here in early July, I flew from Saskatoon to Toronto to London to Moscow, arriving in the Russian capital at 3:45 in the afternoon.

Unfortunately, the departure time of the final leg of my journey – from Domodedovo Airport in Moscow to Magnitogorsk – had been pushed back five-and-a-half hours, from six to eleven-thirty p.m., thanks to the new summer travel schedule. As Russia hiccups its way along the path towards capitalism the airlines are constantly short of planes, and as a result they need to be in service virtually twenty-four hours a day. On the smaller, less-travelled routes, they commonly cancel some flights and add others based on aircraft availability. So the last thing I needed was the first thing that happened to me – a lengthy layover in the Russian capital. Factoring in the two-hour time change from Moscow to Magnitogorsk, by the time Siberian Airlines Flight No. 12 touched down, it was three-thirty in the morning.

One hour later, in the pitch dark, I surveyed as well as I could my new home, where my wife, Linda, and I would live until the end of the hockey season. My new team wanted me on the ice bright and early that same day, so I had a choice – sleep for ninety minutes or stay up and plod through without sleep. I opted for a quick catnap and then walked from my apartment to the arena, wondering for the first time (but probably not for the last), What am I doing here?

I'm fifty-seven years old. I've coached Canada's national team through three Winter Olympic Games. I've had two turns as a head coach in the NHL (with the Calgary Flames and the Columbus Blue Jackets). I spent the past two years in the comparatively stable world of the German Elite League, coaching in Hamburg. And when the Russians called I'd had a job lined up in Helsinki, Finland, for the year.

Even though my contract with Magnitogorsk was negotiated months ago, I really don't know much about what I've let myself in for. I don't know my assistant coaches; I don't know the language; and, with one or two exceptions, I don't know the players.

I'm going into this exercise cold turkey, and even though it's July, it's a grey, cold day – perfect hockey weather, in other words. From the outside, the arena matches the weather – and my mood. It's common in Russia for a building that's only fifteen to twenty years old (and ought to be in relatively decent shape) to be deteriorating far faster than it should. Under the former political regime money would often be allocated for construction, but nothing was ever set aside for maintenance, so no maintenance would be done. It's 8:15 a.m. on my first day on the job and the first group of players is scheduled to go on the ice at ten. If this were an NHL practice, everybody would be here already – trainers, equipment managers, and naturally the players as well. Instead, it's just me and a couple of "key" ladies, one of whom recognized me and let me in the door.

Years ago, I had a Russian player with the Calgary Flames named Sergei Makarov, who was a member of the famous KLM line. The Soviets perennially won the world championships in that era, and Makarov had always been a key contributor. He eventually came to the NHL at the age of thirty-one, along with the other members of his "unit" – Igor Larionov, Vladimir Krutov, Alexei Kasatonov, and Slava Fetisov. When he played for me, I could never get used to the fact that Makarov would do exactly what my team was doing right now. He would appear just before practice began and then would be gone minutes after training was completed. I thought that was just Sergei's way. Now I'm beginning to suspect that this may actually be the

Russian way. We'll see if that changes over the course of the season.

Eventually, everybody drifted in, beginning with my new coaching colleagues. There's Fedor Kanareykin, my number one assistant, who speaks a little English. Then there are the three Viktors – Viktor Korolev, Viktor Suchov, and Viktor Gudzik – none of whom speaks a word of English. This could be challenging.

Soon after I took the job, I bought a set of Berlitz language tapes and picked up a few rudimentary Russian expressions – hello, goodbye, thank you, etc. etc.

In the main, though, I plan to coach in English, and to do that I'm going to need to "pre-ice" all our practices. By that I simply mean that I'll go over the drills with the Russian assistant coaches first and then they can translate for me. As I stepped on the ice, I had only one thought in my mind – Don't fall on your ass, Kinger! – because wouldn't that be an inspired beginning?

So I blew the whistle and called the players over to the coaching board, just as I'd done a thousand other times during my coaching career. I thought I'd start with something easy – a simple drill to warm up the goalies that I thought was guaranteed foolproof.

Wrong. Apparently, even the simplest drills can go awry when you're dealing with a language barrier. Thirty seconds into my first drill, I had to blow the whistle to stop the play, straighten it out, and start all over again. Ninety minutes later, near the end of practice, a handful of players were on their knees, between repetitions, gasping for breath.

Our view of Russian athletes, perhaps coloured by too many *Rocky* movies, is that they are, if nothing else, fitter than their North American counterparts. Later I would learn that Russian players treat training camp the way NHL players of the Gordie Howe era once did – as a means of gradually playing themselves into shape – but my first impression was less than kind.

Never would I have expected Russian players to be so bagged after just one on-ice session. In all, I had four on-ice sessions that day, before wandering back to my apartment. I had travelled through twelve time zones and slept for ninety minutes out of thirty-six hours, but fuelled by the adrenalin, the jet lag, and the stimulation of my new surroundings, I found myself wide awake when, by all rights, I should be dead to the world. As I lay there making a series of mental notes, I felt a wide range of emotions – from sadness at leaving behind the people I love to excitement at the prospect of entering the closely guarded world of Russian hockey. It was one of the hardest days of my life coaching – but a great day too. I was so fired up to be on the ice with Russian players, running these guys through drills and seeing what they've got. Up until then the notion of coaching in Russia had been just an abstract idea. Now it was my new reality.

July 7

Magnitogorsk is a city of about 400,000 people in the foothills of the Ural Mountains, not far from the Kazakhstan border and about two-and-a-half hours by airplane south and east of Moscow. Technically, we're just west of the Siberian plain.

Just how I ended up here – voluntarily – requires a brief explanation. Back on May 1, I'd agreed to take a job coaching one of the top teams in Finland, IFK Helsinki. IFK had fired their coach in the middle of the playoffs and their general manager, a former national team coach himself, Pentti Matakainen, had taken over until the end of the year. Three days after I'd agreed to take the job in Helsinki, I took a call from a well-known player agent named Serge Levin, who said there was a team in Russia interested in hiring a North American head coach. They thought they had something arranged with Barry Smith, a Detroit Red Wings' assistant, but the deal had fallen through and they were looking again. Would I be interested?

In January I had spoken briefly with Serge about Russia, and had said, "Yeah, it'd be great, I'd be interested," but he didn't follow up and so I didn't think anything more of it. Suddenly, after all this time, he called with more details.

The team, he said, was Magnitogorsk, and because I followed the league, I knew they were a competitive club. He outlined how they travelled and who some of their players were. I quickly got on the computer and checked them out, and after about two or three hours, I realized, Hmmm, this could be very, very interesting.

So I said to Linda, "I wonder how IFK would react to this proposal?" We thought about it and talked about it, and it just seemed as if it could be a once-in-a-lifetime opportunity. When you get to be a little bit older in the coaching profession, you have to go year by year. It isn't as if I was forty-five years old any more, when waiting for one season, and fulfilling my contractual obligation in Finland, wouldn't be that big a deal.

This was a good Russian team, and financially there was quite a difference in salary too. So I picked up the phone and called GM Pentti Matakainen and president Harri Tuomo and explained how the opportunity had come up. I told them that I'd really like to consider the Russian offer, even though I'd signed in Helsinki already. Naturally, they didn't want to make a change because they'd already made the news of my hire public, but they did agree to talk to me about it in Vienna, which was hosting the 2005 world hockey championship.

By then I was already home from Europe for the summer, so I flew over to Vienna. The Russians met me, en masse, at the airport and my first thoughts were, They're so emotional, and so excited about the possibility of hiring this North American coach, and they don't always shake hands, they lay kisses on you. I was hoping for hugs but no kisses.

The scene at the airport was absolutely chaotic. A whole troop of people was there to meet me, one of whom was Mark Gandler, the agent for a lot of Russian hockey players, including Alexei Yashin. Mark didn't broker the deal, but because he spoke English and the Russians needed somebody to translate, he'd volunteered to handle the job for a day or so. We went right from the airport to the Renaissance Hotel. After travelling all night and most of that day, I expected to go up to my room and have a little quiet time before we met to talk contract. But they had other ideas. They helped me take my luggage up to my room and then we went right back down to the lobby of the hotel to start the negotiations.

Now picture this: we were smack in the middle of a major Vienna hotel during the world hockey championships, with people going back and forth all the time and people I knew waving at me – and meanwhile, I'm trying to talk to these Russians in a foreign language about a complicated contract. Gennady Velichkin, the general manager, was talking on his cellphone virtually the entire time. Then someone else's cellphone would ring and they'd hand it to him and now he's got two cellphone conversations going simultaneously. Oleg Kuprianov, the assistant general manager, is a high, high energy guy and he also spoke a little English, so he was trying to practise his English on me – on critical issues in the negotiations – and I couldn't understand a word. So I was saying, "Use the translator, use the translator!" Everybody was smoking. It was chaos.

Oleg also carried this little black bag full of U.S. dollars. The first question he asked me was, "Where are your receipts?" because he wanted to pay me my travel expenses immediately. I said, "Oleg, can we do that tomorrow, I just got off the plane!" But he really wanted to get it done right there and then – to pay my expenses, in U.S. cash, in the middle of a hotel lobby.

They had a contract out, on the coffee table, ready for me to sign. I was trying to explain, through Mark, that I really couldn't sign anything until I could get my IFK contract properly terminated. When Mark explained this, all of a sudden things went really quiet. I could sense Velichkin was starting to get nervous. They had lost Barry

Smith already when they thought they had him and now I could see him thinking, Is this going to happen to us again?

But they backed off long enough for me to meet with Harri Tuomo twice. The IFK were reluctant to make a change; in fact, I wasn't sure if they'd go for it at all. So when I told Velichkin of IFK's position, he called my agent, the two spoke, and then Velichkin handed me the phone. Apparently, the Russians were prepared to do what they always do – throw money at the problem. Velichkin offered to pay IFK a generous fee to release me from my contract and asked that I communicate their proposal to Tuomo. That, apparently, made the difference. Harri wasn't very happy, but he understood that at this stage of my career it was probably a chance that would never come again. He said he didn't want to hire a reluctant coach, but he also said that they'd be seeking further monetary compensation if possible. Nowadays, everyone in hockey seems to think the Russians have deep pockets.

Later that same evening, just before supper, the contract appeared again and this time I was able to sign it right there at the dinner table. As soon as that happened, the glasses came out. Now, I'm not much of a drinker, but you had to toast the new contract, so they brought out the vodka bottle, which I never drink, and it wasn't a shot glass full either. It was an enormous goblet, about the size of a water glass.

That night, I remember going back to my room and reflecting on the whole situation. Now I was really committed to Russia. Before, it was a nice-to-do thing, a possibility. Now it was real.

Then I started to think, Geez, I've coached a few Russians along the way – and I can't say it's been easy. For the most part, I'd found Russian players to be stubborn. They always wanted to debate everything with you, and now I was about to coach thirty of them. This was going to be very interesting.

Apart from one or two imports we might bring in, I'd be the only foreign content on the team, and so it would require a balancing act.

While I had to bring some new things to the table, I also needed to understand that I wasn't going to drastically change these people or the way they play.

I'd have to be careful about what I attempted to change, and to do it slowly and win their confidence early. Real changes might not occur until the second half of the season. It's not my nature to accept that, but in the end, it may be the way it would have to be.

I remember that when the Russians first came to the NHL, the transition wasn't easy for some of them. Now, all of a sudden, the shoe was on the other foot. Players will tell you that I tend to be fairly stubborn, so over the summer I spent a lot of time thinking, not so much about ice hockey, but about how I could facilitate change. What would be the steps involved in making that happen?

So much of coaching is learning what works with each individual. No matter where you're coaching – in the NHL or in Germany or in Japan, all places that I've previously worked – you have to reach twenty to twenty-five players. Some respond to the carrot. Some respond to the stick. Not everyone is a quick study, but at least when you're dealing with someone in the same language, you eventually learn which buttons to push.

That's a critical part of coaching, but I had to concede that, with some of the Russian players I've coached in the past, I could never even find the button, let alone push it.

In Russia, the rapport between coach and player always seemed different. On the ice, I've watched Russian coaches with their players and it would be a debate, a very active debate. Hands would be waving, people would be pointing, and you could see the players saying, "It wasn't me, it was the other guy" – and the other guy saying, "No way." I've seen that happen many times watching Russian teams train.

In North America, the solution is usually simple: you go have a cup of coffee with a guy, or go for a walk, or skate around the ice and talk to him, or invite him into your office and solve your problems that way. Now it would be difficult to discuss critical issues with a player because I'd have to use a translator.

The words he translates might be the same as the ones I say, but would he be able to communicate my passion or my inflection? Probably not. In some ways, I'd have to become more animated with my hands and my facial expressions so that a player could pick up cues visually. So I told myself, When I'm making a point emphatically, through a translator, the player is going to have to see my face and look into my eyes and sense my body language.

When I coached in Germany I kept catching myself saying, "This is the way we do things in the NHL" – which, of course, is the wrong way to approach things here. Instead, what I needed to do is separate the things I think I can change from the ones I can't – and then laugh at the rest and not let them bother me. I already knew I'd be in for a bit of a shock in terms of the hockey culture. For example, I'd be seeing their doctors sticking needles into people and asking players to take this pill or that pill. Vincent Riendeau, the former St. Louis Blues' goaltender, played for Lada Togliatti and once told me that whenever the team doctor came into the dressing room he'd head the other way – because they were always trying to give him something, a pill or an injection, and they wouldn't tell you what it was all about. To me, it's going to be fascinating to see what questions I do ask and what things I'm prepared to ignore.

July 9

In a few days we'll be on our way to Garmisch-Partenkirchen, Germany, for two weeks of altitude training that should give me a better idea of the kind of team we have. Frankly, after three days on the ice, I'm not that impressed. In my days as Canada's national team coach, I travelled here at least twice a year and became familiar with how things were done in the old days – when it was the Soviet Union, not Russia; when the coaches ruled with an iron fist, not a velvet glove; and when their training schedules were so regimented that by August their teams were in mid-season shape already and our national team had to play close to its best hockey just to keep the games competitive. I stopped coming regularly in 1992 when I started to coach the Calgary Flames, and had since been back only once before – for the 2000 world championships in St. Petersburg. Even then, seeing how the landscape had shifted on every level – politically, economically, socially – was absolutely mind-boggling.

Politically, things started to change in the late 1980s – *glasnost* and *perestroika* were the catchphrases people used to describe the gradual evolution away from Communism towards capitalism. From the time Mikhail Gorbachev came to power in March 1985 to the time he lost power on Christmas Day, 1991, everything changed. Some people compared Moscow of the mid-1990s to Al Capone's Chicago or to the Wild West because of the violence and crime and lawlessness that permeated their evolving and ever-changing society.

From a hockey perspective, lots of things changed as well – and in many ways, times have come almost full circle. Up until the fall of Communism, the only way a Russian player in his prime could come to the NHL was to defect. A handful did so – most prominently, Alexander Mogilny in 1989 – but for the most part it took until the early 1990s before the trickle of Russian players became a bona-fide Russian invasion. Sergei Fedorov was only twenty-one when he walked away from the Goodwill Games in 1990 and right into the Detroit Red Wings' lineup (and seven years later, along with countrymen Igor Larionov, Slava Kozlov, and Vladimir Konstantinov, he would parade the Stanley Cup around Red Square). Pavel Bure came a year later, in 1991, and as a twenty-one-year-old promptly won the NHL's rookie of the year award.

As the NHL's Russian content soared, not many people gave much thought to the downside of that phenomenon – just how the Russian exodus devastated their own internal leagues. For a few years, the Russian Super League consisted of old players and young players – nothing in between. Dmitri Yushkevich, the ex-Leaf, ex-Flyers' defenceman, once told me that his comrades in Cherepovets – the players he grew up with and the ones he left behind when he came to the NHL in 1992 – made so little money in those early days that they'd spend part of their day literally fishing for their supper so that they could feed their families.

Those first tentative steps towards capitalism featured so much upheaval and volatility in their society that it was, frankly, worrisome to me. Chaos reigned in those days, and even now safety was an issue when Linda and I had weighed the pros and cons of taking this job.

This past summer, Norm Maracle, who played in the Detroit Red Wings organization and now plays goal for Avangard Omsk, told me about a wild story that happened just before he arrived to play in Magnitogorsk. During the 2001 season, the team's twenty-five-year-old backup goalie, Sergei Zemchonok, was shot dead while leaving the elevator of his apartment building. Robbery was the motive. Sergei drove a nice car, was always well-dressed, and carried a handbag, which police felt made him a target. The two killers were eventually captured and charged, mostly because their modus operandi mirrored a similar murder-robbery that had taken place in Chelyabinsk. Still, that sort of tale gives you pause.

I was aware too that Valentin Sych, the former president of the federation, was found in a gravel dump, murdered some years ago in a crime that was widely linked to the Russian mafia. It wasn't that Sych himself was involved with the mafia. What happened was, in the early days of the transition away from Communism, the Russian Ice Hockey Federation had no money to run its programs. They were broke. They were desperate. So whenever they left the country, they brought back large quantities of duty-free cigarettes that they could sell to the cigarette brokers, who in turn re-sold them in the markets. Sych wasn't even doing this to enrich himself. He was doing it to fund programs for their kids. But he was treading on dangerous ground, because the cigarette market was controlled by the Russian underworld. They tell me that he didn't even get a warning. They just shot him dead – and delivered a message to the federation, at his expense, to get out of the cigarette business.

So there were issues on any number of levels to ponder – worries about physical violence, and concerns about health and sanitation. Russia, in the summer of 2005, sounded as if it were a significantly different place from the one I was familiar with, which could be both a good thing and a bad thing.

It's one reason why, when Gennady Velichkin asked me today if I wanted to meet our team owner, Viktor Rashnikov, I jumped at the opportunity. Magnitogorsk is a steel city and Rashnikov operates MMK, one of Russia's largest steel companies. They sponsor our team. Rashnikov is said to be worth upwards of US$3 billion – yes, that's $3 *billion* – which would make him the fourteenth or fifteenth wealthiest man in the country. He's one of the oligarchs you hear so much about. Some, like Roman Abramovich, are famous because they own soccer teams like Chelsea; closer to home he also owns Avangard Omsk of the Russian Super League. Others, like Mikhail Khodorkovsky of the Russian state-owned Yukos oil company, are currently in jail for tax evasion. Rashnikov was an engineer who cobbled together the necessary resources in the move from Communism towards capitalism that enabled him and his investors to buy the state-owned steel company at well below market value. In a short period of time the oligarchs became rich beyond all comprehension. They're the J. Paul Gettys and Andrew Carnegies, the William Randolph Hearsts and Andrew Mellons of their era, so the prospect of meeting him fascinated me.

Driving up to the steel factory with Velichkin, I was immediately overwhelmed by its sheer size. It's almost six miles long and runs along the banks of the Ural River forever. The Ural is the boundary between Asia and Europe. As we drew closer we could see smoke billowing over the factory and the surrounding area, two or three different shades of smoke, one of which was bright orange. Velichkin assured me that the plant had made great strides to meet new, tougher ecological standards, but seeing that orange smoke made me wonder. One fact was indisputable: the quality of the air in Magnitogorsk seems typical of most large steel cities circa the 1950s. A steady, ever-present haze has hung over the city ever since I arrived.

Rashnikov's office building lies deep in the recesses of the plant, and was designed to impress. Martha Stewart would find herself at home here – it's a modern, up-to-date suite, with understated but impressive finishing touches. Rashnikov himself is fifty-eight and in great physical shape. Physically, he looks chiselled out of granite. His leadership presence is unmistakable. He commands respect. Even at first blush it was easy to understand how he could emerge as the leader of MMK during a time when there surely had to be competition to assume control of the steel mill's assets. Nowadays he travels the world drumming up business for MMK, but Velichkin told me he attends virtually every home game when he's in town.

In our ninety-minute meeting today, he told me about his expectations for the upcoming year: nothing too onerous, either. For the season to be considered a success, the team needed to finish in the top three, which would put us in the medals. Anything less would be viewed as a failure. In his mind, he financed the team very well, and based on our budget, of about US$22 million, we should be able to reach the Super League semifinals. I found him to be very intense and unbelievably focused. There was no small talk. There was no "Great to see you, how are you, how's your family, do you have a wife?" It was all business. There was no fooling around. "This is what we spend on the team. This is what I expect. This is what I want." And that was it.

Our budget is actually higher than the $21.5 million salary-cap floor negotiated by the NHL in the last collective bargaining agreement. In the year of the NHL lockout, the highest-spending team in Russia was Ak Bars Kazan, with a budget of $60 to $70 million. They were the New York Rangers of the Super League, and they didn't win anything either. As the economy gradually improved, the Russian Super League became the highest-paying league outside the NHL. Because the tax laws are less restrictive, some players – at the top end – can make more by playing here than in the NHL. Vityaz, one of the new expansion teams in the league this year, reportedly offered Alexei Zhamnov and Vladimir Malakhov US$3 million per year as a net salary – the equivalent of about $5 million in the NHL. Both turned them down. There are a number of prominent NHL players in Russian training camps right now – Pavel Datsyuk, Ilya Kovalchuk, and with us, Evgeny Malkin – who still have to decide where they want to play this year, here or in the NHL.

For the high-end guys, the money will be roughly comparable once they factor in the tax advantages of playing in Russia, so it'll mostly be a lifestyle decision. Do they want to stay home, playing in front of friends and family? Or will they want to play in the NHL, still the best league in the world? It will be interesting to see how it all unfolds.

After the meeting with Rashnikov, Velichkin invited me to his house for dinner, along with Fedor Kanareykin, my number one assistant. Now, I'm not sure what I expected to see, because my first impression of Magnitogorsk was of a modest, blue-collar city. So it came as a shock to me when we pulled up in front of his house, in a gated community that could have been in Phoenix or Miami or any other upper-class American suburb. It wasn't a house, it was practically a castle, and looked as if it came right out of *Architectural Digest*.

Outside in the garden, there was a waterfall, indirect lighting on the trees, and a fish pond. Three of our executives – Velichkin, Oleg Kuprianov (the man with the black bag full of U.S. currency), and Vladimir Aleko, another one of our financial people – all live side by side in this subdivision. There were hot tubs. There was a sauna and a big-screen satellite television and a pool table. I've been in the homes of many NHL general managers and this was as, or more, impressive.

The Velichkins had invited three other families over for dinner, so for me this was an important ice-breaker, a chance to observe some of my new colleagues in a social environment, away from the rink. Velichkin's teams have done very well over the years – they were champions in both 1999 and 2000. They expected to win, and the rewards for winning were obviously great. But the meeting with Rashnikov and now the dinner with Velichkin drove home another point – that there may also be a price to pay for failure. And in my experience it's usually the coach, not the GM, who pays that price. If nothing else, the NHL and the Russian Super League seem to have that in common.

July 10

One of the things that intrigued me most about my upcoming adventure was the knowledge that we'd decamp almost immediately for Garmisch-Partenkirchen, a beautiful village in the Alps. Today we arrived and checked into the Renaissance Riesersee Hotel, a gorgeous five-star resort. The idea was to spend the most gruelling part of our summer preparation in one of the most beautiful places on earth, in the hopes that it would make the task of getting into shape less onerous. We'd be here for twelve days, with thirty-four players and a staff of ten. Upon arrival, every player received a rental mountain bike for his use, but most players preferred to take the shuttle bus down the mountain to the Olympic Ice Stadium in Garmisch for our two-a-day on-ice workouts, plus one off-ice fitness session. The costs seemed extraordinarily high, and once again I was amazed at the apparently endless supply of money to operate this team. We lack for nothing, and if we do need something the solution is to open up Oleg Kuprianov's ever-present black bag and pay cash.

Camp is demanding, which is a good thing because you can really see a player's character start to emerge under this sort of regimen. Since training camp is nine weeks long, I'd take the first ten days or so to do a lot of exercises that would give me a sense of my team and its talent level and, most importantly, who might be the most influential guys in the group. I also wanted to evaluate how competitive these guys were. Frankly, my first reaction was that a lot of these players might be quite skilled, but too many of them were out of shape. I found a real dichotomy there – that we were operating a camp like an NHL team, but we had mostly high-end AHL-type players.

The single most obvious exception is Evgeny Malkin, who stands out every day because there are simply not a lot of players like him. The Pittsburgh Penguins selected Malkin second overall in the 2004 NHL entry draft, just behind another Russian player, Alexander Ovechkin, who went to the Washington Capitals as number one overall. And Magnitogorsk is Malkin's hometown, which makes him even more valuable to the team. He has a chance to be the best player in our league this year, and pretty soon the tug-of-war for his services is going to start in earnest. It looked as if the NHL lockout was just about to end and you could be sure that someone like Malkin would be attractive to Pittsburgh, which finished dead last in the NHL last season and would need somebody to generate some excitement.

From what I can tell, Malkin is the real thing too. Sometimes there's a lot of hoopla about a guy who turns out to be just an average player. Malkin is not that. Unquestionably, he's going to be a great player. He's about six-foot-three and very linear in terms of build. Athletically, he's extremely gifted. Not only is he a great hockey player, but he's also our best soccer player and an incredible tennis player. His body awareness is something to behold. He can be graceful, but just at the right moment he can be explosive as well. In one-on-one drills he simply evaporates as he goes past a defender. And as with all great players, his eyes are always up and he sees the game one or two plays ahead at all times.

Anatoli Tarasov, the legendary Russian coach, used to say that in the game someone must "mastermind" the pass – meaning that sometimes a player needed to skate off the puck and let the "holes" or "windows" open to create a passing opportunity for the puck carrier at precisely the right time. It's a difficult concept to absorb and an almost impossible concept to teach. It's that sixth sense that enabled scorers such as Mike Bossy and Brett Hull to materialize in the right place at the right time, over and over again. Malkin can do that very well, but he also has the ability to pass the puck with great precision. He disguises his intentions so well that his passes are Wayne Gretzky-like.

Probably what I like best about Malkin is that he loves his work. Sometimes Russian players can be extremely dour. Malkin smiles all the time. He seems to enjoy practice. He loves to compete. He plays the game with tempo. He's unselfish. Most importantly, he does what all great players do: he can see things happen in front of him while sensing the pressure coming from behind – which tells him how much time he has to make his play. The key for him will be dealing with all the attention that is sure to come his way – and will this adversely affect his opinion of himself?

July 12

Travis Scott, our import goalie and for now the only other Canadian in the organization, arrived in Germany today and all eyes were on him. Magnitogorsk has had problems with goaltending in the past, although not during the lockout after they signed Evgeny Nabokov of the San Jose Sharks for a year. But Nabokov went back to the NHL, so we needed to get somebody else in. We tried to get Jean-Sébastien Aubin to make a commitment, and actually waited two or three weeks longer than we wanted. But then it became clear that he was still hoping to stay in the NHL, signing with Toronto to play on their farm team, so finally we had to turn the page. We had a list of other goalies, and Travis Scott, who's from the Ottawa area, was at the top of the list of guys who'd been really consistent at the American Hockey League level. He'd played one NHL game for the Los Angeles Kings in the 2000-01 season, but had mostly played in the minor leagues throughout his career.

The Super League permits you to use three imports per team per season, and we knew right from the start that we'd use up one of those spots on a goalie. For the last two years Travis had played in the Florida Panthers' system for their AHL team in San Antonio. Year in and year out he'd produced a respectable goals-against-average and a consistently high save percentage in the AHL, even though he often played for teams that were just average or quite poor. And of course, I did a lot of research on Travis. I phoned Dave Pryor, the Washington goaltender coach. I phoned François Allaire, the goaltending guru to Patrick Roy and J.S. Giguère and other goalies. I also called my former assistant Guy Charron, who did some work with Florida's farm team last year because of the lockout. And everybody told me the same thing: he's a very unorthodox goalie. He doesn't play the butterfly style. He doesn't make the same save twice the same way, but he stops the puck. As a coach, that's what matters the most – that he stops the puck.

Travis and his family have lived a bit of a nomadic existence, which is what happens to players just on the cusp of making it to the NHL, but the places he's been to (Baton Rouge, Worcester, Lowell, Manchester, San Antonio) couldn't possibly prepare him for the culture shock of coming to Magnitogorsk. So in order to ease his transition, we didn't ask him to report with the rest of the team in early July; we just told him to join our team here in Garmisch-Partenkirchen so that he could get a chance to meet the guys and to decide if he really wanted to do this. Because, frankly, the last thing you want is to commit to someone in a key position like goal and then discover afterwards that they hate it, or aren't prepared to stick it out, because then you're stuck.

Our backup goalie is Konstantin Simchuk, and he's a real character. He was born in Kiev, but speaks English very well and, like Travis, has been something of a hockey nomad. He's thirty-one, and three years ago he too realized that he wasn't going to make it to the NHL, after years of trying. He played mostly in the low minor leagues – Tacoma, Las Vegas, Bakersfield, Port Huron, Knoxville, San Diego, and Fort Wayne. In 2002 he came back to Russia and played for Ufa Salavat Yulaev for two years, and then moved on to Novosibirsk before coming to Magnitogorsk last year.

Simchuk is a chatterbox, so I asked him why it's so hard to get the rest of our players to talk in practice. We could eliminate a great deal of hesitation in our defensive play if the players would simply talk on the ice. Konstantin wished me luck in trying to change that mindset. He said it was part of the Russian culture: that they tended to be quiet on the outside, even though they may be overflowing with feelings on the inside; and that the tendency to internalize their emotions dated back to the Soviet days when people learned to fend for themselves. Konstantin may be the most vocal goalie I've ever coached, and his feedback gave me something to think about. Maybe we can convince our small group of veteran players, some of whom do speak English and have played in North America before, to start talking on the ice. If they do, the younger players might follow.

July 24

Camp in Garmisch ended yesterday and things are starting to come into focus for me. We flew back to Russia today and landed at Domodedovo Airport, where we spent two hours jammed into a hall meant for two hundred people, not the seven or eight hundred who were actually crammed in there. It was a mess. It was a Sunday and all the charter flights were arriving at the same time, but even so, most of the passport booths were unmanned. People started yelling and complaining, which of course did no good; passport control just phoned for more security, which only increased the size of the crowd and added to the general level of frustration. The next day a lengthy article in the Moscow paper documented the passport control problems and suggested that they were still operating as if it were the Soviet Union – where the solution was to produce a greater security presence to make the problem go away. In the new Russia, that doesn't work. For the second time coming into Magnitogorsk, we arrive at four a.m. By the time we get to our apartments, the sun is sneaking over the horizon.

July 27

Normally an NHL team may play its first exhibition game a week into training camp, but now that we're back in Magnitogorsk, we're just about to begin our pre-season competition schedule and it's clear that the players are getting anxious to play. We'll open with two games against Molot Perm, the last-place team from a year ago. By the looks of it, they'll struggle again. In the opener we won 9-0; it looked too much like a Harlem Globetrotters–Washington Generals' game. We had the puck the whole time and after a while started to become too cute with it. Overall, it was mostly a waste of time.

For the rematch I dressed only fifteen players, including six rookies, and that made the second game more of a contest. It finished 2-2 and we were in the penalty box all night, which gave us a chance to work on our penalty-killing. Malkin, especially, got a little too individual and twice got caught with good hits. Both Alexander Boikov and Vladislav Boulin, who have extensive North American experience, came to Malkin's defence, and delivered the message that "You don't take liberties with our top player."

Right now I'm mostly using Boikov to help me translate. Boikov played ten NHL games for the Nashville Predators in their first two seasons and spent eleven years altogether in North America, from the time he was a junior playing for the Victoria Cougars of the Western Hockey League until three years ago when he first joined Magnitogorsk. His English is good, but translation is an art and I can tell it's not easy for him. As a coach, over the years you develop almost a separate hockey language that's practically impossible to translate. Many of the descriptive cue words or phrases you use – such as "ride the passer" or "get close and stay close" – can clarify a difficult concept to an English-speaking listener; unfortunately, they can't be translated in their proper context from English to Russian and are therefore almost unusable to me now. I'm thinking there may be some truth to the expression "A picture is worth a thousand words" and plan to introduce video analysis soon. I've broken down the tape of the two games against Molot Perm and I'm waiting to see how that's received.

Right now our team is at the rink almost every day, and throughout the season they'll be fed, up to three times a day, in our own cafeteria. This is completely new to me and unlike anything you'd see in the NHL. Usually about two-thirds of our team will come in early in the morning, eat their breakfast at the rink, then go down to the dressing room to do their stretching and go on the ice. There's a full breakfast menu – porridge and fried eggs, fish and cold meats, and all kinds of other things. Then, after morning practice, lunch is served buffet-style. If we have an afternoon practice, there's a supper meal as well. Players can come for a meal or not; it's their choice. There's a good variety and it's well-prepared.

I don't think of myself as a picky eater, but there are some things I'm having a hard time trying to digest. For lunch, there are always one or two types of soups that are good. Then we have two or three main courses – usually a fish, beef, or pork main course, with potatoes or rice.

Then they often serve fish heads. This, to me, is just unbelievable. What they do with the fish heads is this: they get a bowl, scoop out the fish head from this big hot pot full of broth, use their fingers or burrow into it with their teeth right up to where the brain of the fish would be, and then pull this stuff out and eat it. It's disgusting. Honestly, I'm at the end of the table and I just turn and face the other way.

Another thing I've run across is horse milk. Now, I like milk and I drink a lot of milk, but I think horses are for riding or betting on, not for milking. Horse milk is thicker than cow's milk, so you have to shake the bottle because all the sediment sinks to the bottom. The water looks kind of milky and greyish and you can almost see through it. The first time I had it I didn't know it was horse milk, so I shook it up and I tried some and ugh, it just was not to my taste.

July 28

My wife, Linda, won't join me for another month, and today it's just as well she isn't here because I'm having water problems in our apartment. It isn't what you'd think, either. The hot water works; it's the cold water that doesn't, and as a result my morning showers are scalding. If this continues I may have to shower at the arena. As well, the toilets operate on cold water, so you can't flush the thing unless you go to the kitchen (where, inexplicably, the cold water *is* working) and carry two pails of water back and forth to the bathroom. I found out later that someone in our apartment block needed to replace some old pipe. Unlike North America, where someone would come to your door to tell you that your water is being turned off, you're left to discover this for yourself.

Our apartment is small, but very clean. It's owned and was recently renovated by the team and they make it available to whoever is coaching that year. It's fully furnished, there's satellite television, and they'll provide any other amenities we might eventually require.

Unlike Germany, where there are restaurants and coffee shops everywhere, there don't appear to be many here. On the other hand, the grocery stores are pretty good. In the 1980s, when I used to come to Russia, the shop shelves were bare. It was a shortage economy, with long lines for dairy products. People received ration cards for items in short supply, of which there were plenty. When the NHL wives of Russian players first arrived in North America they'd fill their shopping carts with food, fearing that if they came back tomorrow the shelves would be empty. They had to be told that there would always be steak or chicken or fish available – today, tomorrow, next week.

As part of my contract I had access to a car, but I turned it down, first of all because when I got over here I saw how they drive – crazy. Then I saw some of the streets, and they were not well marked. Some have lane markings; others don't. Some of the cars they drive are so decrepit that it doesn't matter if they sideswipe somebody else. It's just another ding in the car. They're always in a hurry and drive far too fast, and seat belts have often been removed or disengaged.

Besides, I live in an apartment that's almost right across the street from the rink. They told me that if I didn't want a car, they'd provide me with a driver at any time. I also found out that taxis are really cheap. You can go downtown for a dollar.

Plus, I didn't want the complication of worrying about a car and wondering if it would still be there in the morning. Auto theft is a major problem here. There are three outdoor hockey rinks in our neighbourhood and two of them have been turned into parking lots. The old rink shack, where people would change into their skates, is used by a security guard who sits there twenty-four hours a day and watches. In effect, these outdoor rinks have become parking compounds for cars in the summer. Cars are stolen so frequently over here that few people would park their car outside their apartment; it could be gone the next morning or broken into. Instead, they pay to park a block away and pick up their car in the morning at the compound. Then they drive to work and drop it off again at night.

July 29

We held our first video meeting today to review the games with Molot Perm. I used a laser light pencil to highlight a player or play, an approach the players had never seen before. Afterwards, Igor Mouraviev, my off-ice translator, told me that the presentation had received rave reviews. Russian coaches don't generally use videotape as an instructional aid. We showed eleven clips and the English-speaking players said the session clarified a lot of things for them. The important thing for me was to keep the sessions short and to end each one with three or four positive clips.

July 30

We're on the bus to Ufa to play a four-team tournament against some of the better teams in the league, including the host, Salavat Yulaev, plus Ak Bars Kazan and Lada Togliatti. Our trip took us alongside the Ural Mountains for about two hours, during which we passed small towns that exist as if in a time warp. The buildings are old and run down, but at the point where the highway passed through there'd be a modern gas bar or the Russian equivalent to a convenience store. Cattle and sheep roamed through the towns and twice we needed to stop or slow down to let the cattle pass. Two dead cows were lying on the roadside and it was clear that someone had run them over at night. Others had crowded into the roadside bus shelters, seeking relief from the sun. We passed other buses where the bus would stop and men, women, and children would sprint into the bushes to relieve themselves, since there are no bathrooms on the buses and no rest stops on the rural highways.

Ufa itself is built along the Belya River and is a beautiful place, with many parks and natural stands of trees. It's clean, too. It's named after Salavat Yulaev, a famous leader, who co-authored a rebellion against Czarina Yekatharina II some two hundred years ago. The Czarina's armies won, and Yulaev died in a prison on an island in the Baltic Sea. His co-conspirator was taken to Red Square in Moscow, where he was executed by being drawn and quartered. Losers, in Russia, apparently pay a heavy price, something to keep in mind as the season moves along.

August 1

We played Lada today in the Ufa tournament. They were one of the best teams in the league last season, so it finally gave me a chance to see how our team might look this season. Training camp and our two wins over Molot Perm didn't leave me with a good first impression, but today we competed hard, and tied 1-1. On the way back to the hotel our bus passed a controlled intersection, where half-a-dozen gypsy children, aged eight or nine or ten, were standing on the white line in the middle of the road. Whenever the cars stopped for a red light, these children would beg for money by tapping on the car windows. Some didn't have any shoes and all were very poorly dressed. It was a striking contrast. Here we were, on a bus with hockey players making a small fortune by Russian standards, and there were these poor children, wearing threadbare clothes and sorry, hangdog expressions on their faces. It was a reality check, and seemed to make a sobering impression on everyone, not just me.

August 3

Today, in the Ufa tournament final, we tied the game 3-3 in regulation and then lost the championship in a shootout. A few days earlier, in the middle of the tournament, three of our players – our goalie, Konstantin Simchuk, plus Sergei Arekaev and Yuri Dobryishkin – had come up to me and asked, "When the tournament's over, there's a direct flight from Ufa to Moscow, can we take it?" They wanted to go home for a few days to visit their families, and I said no problem, since we were planning to give them two days off anyway. So they booked their flights, but unbeknownst to me the flights were leaving rather close to the end of the game. When the game was over they had to head right to the airport, because the timing was going to be close. The problem was I didn't know when their flights were, only that they were going to leave right after the game. So, there we were, in the final game of the tournament, and it goes into overtime. That didn't decide anything, so now we're heading into a shootout. Naturally, the linesman skated over and gave me the card to fill out with my five shooters. Now, my first thought was to put Simchuk in because he'd been better than Travis Scott on breakaways in practice, but I thought, No, I'll leave Scott in because he's played pretty well in the game.

But I did list the other two players heading to Moscow, Dobryishkin and Arekaev, and after the referee signed the card I read off the names. Suddenly, there was a murmur on the bench. I could hear the players talking and see them waving their hands, but I didn't know what they were saying. It turned out that, as soon as regulation time ended, Dobryishkin and Arekaev had gone straight to the dressing room, taken off their equipment, and jumped in a cab to the airport because they didn't want to miss their flights. The shootout was about to start, and they were already gone. So I called the referee over and tried to explain: "Look, I put these two guys on the list, but they're no longer dressed." Thankfully, the referee let me make a change. Otherwise, I was thinking, Am I down to three shooters instead of five in the shootout? Have I really screwed up my debut in this league so badly? Geez, that was funny. Afterwards, I thought, I've got lots to learn about these guys over here.

August 4

Now that the Ufa tournament is over, it's time to make some player decisions. Right now we're carrying almost six complete five-man units, and that's too many. I've seen seven or eight teams so far and we all look about the same. We have a lot of journeymen Russian players that are real cute and real slick. They look like a million bucks going down the ice – until they get into the difficult areas where you have to pay the price to score, and then they have no idea what to do. You can see why their stats are as minuscule as they are. You can see why some of them can't play in the NHL. They've got skill, but they don't have the grit and they don't have the ability to finish. Their game is not a practical game for the NHL. So far, I can see why a lot of our forwards might have trouble in leagues that are really physical. They're much better suited for the game over here.

The other thing you see is a real shortage of defencemen. We don't have a lot of high-quality, passing defencemen. Every team we've played so far has pretty mobile guys with pretty decent size, yet their passing skills are good but not exceptional. They're better than they are in North America, but by the standards of international hockey, they're not great passers.

In the end, we decide to let three players go – the Makarov brothers, Dmitri and Konstantin, plus Sergei Piskunov. All three were having problems with their weight and weren't competitive enough for our team. This was our first cut, and our first practice with the three players gone went very well. It seemed as if the remaining players got the message. When you let three returning players go so early in camp, it represents a good reality check for everyone else.

August 7

My life just got a whole lot easier; two familiar faces (and long-serving members of the Toronto Maple Leafs) have turned up on my doorstep. First we landed a player I'd been after for months, Dmitri Yushkevich, who played in Cherepovets last year. Yushkevich played seven years for the Maple Leafs between 1995 and 2002 and it's easy to see, even at this advanced stage of his career, why their former general manager, Cliff Fletcher, gave up a first-round draft choice to Philadelphia to get him. He's a warrior, in every sense of the word. Then, on the same day as Yushkevich arrived, we learned that Igor Korolev was coming as well. Korolev played four seasons in Toronto from 1997 to 2001 and didn't have as much of an impact on the Leafs as Yushkevich did (although he did score twenty goals for them in the 1999-00 season, not a bad number for a checking centre). In all, Yushkevich played 786 career games in the NHL, Korolev 795, and I can't even begin to tell you how valuable all that experience will be for me. For one thing, both speak excellent English. For another, they're both familiar with the teaching concepts we use in North America. For a third, they're both well-respected by their peers. Yushkevich is thirty-three; Korolev thirty-five. By Russian standards, that makes them old – too old, in fact, for our team's management. Or at least, they were at the beginning of the summer.

Back when they hired me, I talked about adding both players and was told simply, "Nyet, nyet, we can't have those two guys." They'd both had knee problems throughout their NHL careers; they'd been banged up because they really competed and paid a dear price to play in the NHL. Finally, after a month of nagging, I convinced them that we needed one more defenceman, so we signed Yushkevich. But he had an out-clause in his contract whereby, if he could get an NHL opportunity, he could go there instead – and that's what he wanted to do. So he didn't join us on June 28, the way all the other players did. He came today, right when he said he would if he ran out of NHL options.

When he walked into the dressing room, wow! Guys just stopped in their tracks, first because he's really well built, and second because he walked with a pronounced limp in his right leg. He's had two major operations on his right knee. But all through his NHL career, Dmitri always played hurt. Coaches said to me,

"Yushkevich, I love the guy, because he plays hurt" – probably at the expense of shortening his career. He's about as close to a one-legged player as you can get.

The first four days he was here we were going through a really intense off-ice training program, which included a lot of plyometric hurdle jumps. Finally I said to him, "Dmitri, what are you doing this for? It's got to be hard on your knee." He said, "I'm taking this anti-inflammatory all the time because it's really bothering me." So I said, "Why didn't you tell me?" He answered: "Because I've just arrived. All the other guys have been here a month and a half. I don't want to be an exception." I said, "Well, as of right now, you are an exception." I met with our doctor, who said it was ridiculous that he was trying to do these plyometric drills. So now when we do bounding and those kinds of things, he does weights. He's on the same program, other than that one issue.

But he wouldn't tell me – that's the kind of guy he is. He would not come up and say, "I can't do that." He was just pounding the hell out of his knee. He said, "Skating is relatively easy for me; walking is hard – because my knee aches and swells." Still, he doesn't have good mobility one way. But you can see he's clever about it; he steers people to the other side. He's got all the little tricks that you learn from playing so long. At times, though, he gets into foot races and can't win them because his mobility and quickness have lessened since he was a youngster. And I saw him right at the start of his career, because he played for Russia in the 1992 Olympics against us. Both Dmitri and Igor Korolev played against us and both guys, in their first conversations with me, reminded me of that gold-medal game which they won and we finished second. So I've known them since they were young pups, and Dmitri is just a true warrior and a great competitor. When you see him go down to block a shot when no one else would, it's unbelievable. And already he's made a change in our team; I can see some of the younger guys competing harder because of Dmitri's influence.

As for Igor, his family still lives in Toronto and he's on a Canadian passport now. As a Russian on a Canadian passport he can play for us as a non-import, but his family is going to stay in Canada this year and visit him from time to time. Igor played both centre and wing in the NHL, and he's a complete two-way player. He had pretty decent numbers in the NHL, a guy who adds something to your offence. When you look at his total – fourteen, fifteen, sixteen goals a season – you think, There must have been some important ones for the team there. Plus, he was a checking centre, so he could play against anyone and do the job defensively. He's a real character guy. He played last year in Yaroslav, and the reason I wanted him so badly was a recommendation from Paul Henry, who was a long-time scout for the Canadian national team when I was there. Last year, during the lockout, Paul did some sport psychology work in Yaroslav. He knows the Leafs' Nikolai Antropov pretty well, so during the lockout, when Antropov was playing in Yaroslav, Paul really helped him perform. Paul told me, "You've got to get Korolev because this guy is unbelievable." He said that Igor did all the translation in practice for the team's Finnish coach. He talked about what a great faceoff guy he was, how hard he competed, and how well he played in the playoffs. So I talked and talked until I was blue in the face about how we needed to get Igor, but couldn't convince them.

Then everything changed about two months later. Igor was supposed to report to Yaroslav in early August – and that really rankled Vladimir Yurzinov, who was coaching there. He wanted him over there at the same time as everybody else, with no exceptions. Then Igor was delayed by some paperwork on his visa and would be reporting even later still. Apparently, that was too much for Yurzinov. So his agent, Mark Gandler, suddenly phoned me and said, "They're making so much static for him that I don't think Igor should go there." I'd talked to Mark all summer long and he knew how I felt about Korolev. So he asked: "Can you try to talk to your management one more time?" By then we were into training camp and I could see that our depth at centre ice was going to be a problem. Even with Korolev we were pretty thin at centre and everybody could see it, so this time, they said, "Fine, the price is right, let's sign Korolev." Was I ever pumped! I couldn't wait for him to get here. All of a sudden, everything changed. We get Yushkevich one day and two days later, Korolev arrived too. Manna from heaven.

August 8

I run every day. A week ago today, while we were in Ufa, marked my eighteenth consecutive year of running without missing a single day. Now, a lot of people who run seriously say they run every day, but I mean it literally. I've run with colds and I've run with the flu. I've run when it was thirty degrees above zero and I've run when it was thirty degrees below. I ran the day I had surgery to remove a carcinoma from my face (after the doctor told me I shouldn't and really couldn't run). I ran the day after I cracked my ribs in Columbus, and that was the closest I ever came to missing a day because I was in so much pain. But the doctor gave me some morphine that night, and the next day I told Linda: "I can't feel a thing." She tried to dissuade me for hours, but compromised by coming out with me on the run. I was bent over like an old man, limping down the road, but stubbornly, stupidly, I got in my run that day. The next day I was really sore, but Linda wrapped my ribs so that I wouldn't breathe as deeply and I ran like that, in big-time pain, for three or four weeks. I've had heel spurs. I've had all the illnesses that everyone else has, but I just do it.

I started in the summer of 1987, in Calgary, in the pre-Olympic year. A friend of mine, George Kingston, who was my assistant on the '84 Olympic team, was a guy who ran all the time, rarely taking a day off. That year we'd go on these long runs – for twelve or thirteen miles at a time, which he considered a jog or a light workout. Meanwhile, I'd be thinking, When are we going to turn around and go back? So on August 1 of that year I decided to see if I could run every day for one complete calendar year. I wanted to do it for myself and I wanted to do it to set an example for the players, so that when I talked about fitness and worked them hard off the ice they'd know I was working hard myself. So I did that for the 1987-88 calendar year and then decided, "I'm not going to stop, I'm just going to keep going." I enjoy it. My wife can't believe how I get up in the morning and am out the door as soon as I have my jogging clothes on. I find running to be therapeutic. I've had some unbelievable runs and seen some unbelievable things over the years, including the time I ran with the Olympic torch in Auld's Cove, Nova Scotia, in the rain, prior to the '88 Olympic Games.

I also believe that your own commitment to fitness helps establish credibility. I'm not asking players to do anything in terms of getting into shape that I'm not prepared to do myself. Now, with some players, that philosophy resonates; it carries weight. Others are less impressed. A lot of them think I'm crazy. A lot of them think I'm too focused. They say, "This is another example of a guy who never lightens up." But I thought it had an impact on our team in 1987-88 – because not a single guy ever grumbled about how hard we worked that year.

So today, as part of our four-day high-intensity training block, we had an eight-kilometre run on a day when the temperature hit thirty degrees – and I ran with the players. I finished in the middle of the pack with a time of forty-three minutes. For some reason, when I run I don't sweat much, so when I crossed the finish line the staff and players waiting there were all surprised that my shirt was so dry, which made an impression on them. For the most part, running represents a distinct challenge here because the sidewalks and streets are just so badly maintained. I've been lucky so far because when I go out, at six-thirty or seven o'clock, it's still light out, and right now I'm trying to find a safe running path. I've come to this conclusion: as the days get shorter and winter approaches, I may have to stop running first thing in the morning and start running after practice. By the time December rolls around, it'll still be dark at eight in the morning and I'm really worried because the sidewalks and roads are in very poor shape. You can be running along on a nice smooth road and all of a sudden it drops off eight inches into gravel and uneven surfaces. The manholes often stick up out of the cement six inches.

August 10

Ever since the Pittsburgh Penguins won the NHL draft lottery and then chose Sidney Crosby with the first pick, everyone around here is getting very nervous about losing Malkin to the NHL. Frankly, we can't afford to let that happen, if the goal is to win a championship this year. Malkin is the best player I've seen in the league this year. I had Eric Lindros in 1992, and all the hype surrounding him sounded an awful lot like the hype surrounding Crosby right now. Lindros played in the Olympics as a nineteen-year-old and won an NHL scoring title as a twenty-two-year-old, but at this stage of his development I'd put Malkin ahead of Lindros at the same age. Pittsburgh senses it too, which is why they desperately want him to leave Russia right now and play alongside Crosby, Mario Lemieux, and the rest of their improving roster this season. That would be a disaster for us.

The newspapers in Moscow are saying we'll definitely lose him for sure.

Ovechkin is already gone. He had a contract to play for Roman Abramovich's team, Avangard Omsk, but opted out to join the Capitals. As negotiations heated up, our team arranged for me to speak to Mario Lemieux directly about the situation. We had an amicable talk on the phone about Malkin and what their timetable for him was. Mario said, "Look, we want to get him over here right away." And I said, "We'd love to see him stay because the team has invested a lot of time in him. This organization has developed him since he was a little guy – and it's quite expensive to develop a player to that point and then only have him for one year."

Now, I couldn't tell Mario in good faith that Malkin wasn't ready for the NHL because he'd seen him play at the 2005 world championships and knew that he was. I did tell Mario that Malkin needed to get stronger and that our fifty-one-game schedule and training philosophy would help him improve in that area. On the phone, Velichkin, our general manager who speaks a little bit of English, told Lemieux that they were building Malkin a *dacha*, a summer house, and were spending US$300,000 on it as a show of our commitment to the importance of this player to our team.

Our management is really stressed. For the past two weeks now, Velichkin has looked like a ghost.

In the end, it will be up to Malkin to decide, in conjunction with his agents from the IMG Group. They told me they wanted him to stay in Russia for three reasons: they felt he could play one year here under a Canadian coach and get introduced to a lot of the things that will happen to him in the NHL; that his chances of making the Olympic team will be much better; and that the money payoff was going to be there as well.

During the negotiations I met with Malkin in my office to discuss his options – a frustrating experience because we had to use a translator and so couldn't get the rapport I'd like. We had a good conversation, but it was quite sterile. I told him, "I've coached a lot of players just like you, who were very good young players." I let him know that I thought he was ready for the NHL. I didn't try to tell him he wasn't ready. But I told him that if he decided to stay, there were some upsides. I talked – with him and with Mario Lemieux as well –

about leadership. I said, "You can develop your skills here and get bigger, stronger, and faster, but I also think you can get a chance to demonstrate leadership with us too." Malkin is perceived as a leader, even by the older players here, because he's got real charisma. That's pivotal – and sometimes quite rare. The older guys really like him and spend a lot of time with him. I know Evgeny has a chance to become a stronger personality than he already is, if he decides to stay. We talked about Crosby already being there, and I said, "If you wait another year, that pressure is off too." There's enough pressure in trying to become an NHL player, let alone competing with another NHL number one pick on the same team. My advice was: "Just take your time and maybe you'll go to the NHL next year and be a better player." If Pittsburgh is patient, they'll have a complete player on their hands, someone who might one day replace Mario.

I'm coming to realize too that one of Malkin's most endearing qualities is his attitude and approach to the game. He's so different from some of the Russian players I've coached in the past. He's upbeat, effervescent, smiling – happy all the time.

We have another young player here whom I've nicknamed The Fish, a guy with a lot of talent but whose personality is completely different from Malkin's. Malkin is vibrant and outgoing. He's always having fun. By contrast, The Fish is dour. He's an introvert. I've had The Fish on one of my top two lines throughout training camp because I'd heard what a skilled player he was, that he was an NHL draft choice, and I've been impressed with what I've seen so far. As much as possible, I'm trying to converse with players so that I can get to know them better, but The Fish is a tough nut to crack. There's no eye contact with him and no change of expression – ever. He played well in the Ufa tournament, but whenever he'd score a goal and the guys would give him a pat on the back, there'd be no reaction. He's never happy, he's never sad. He just seems cold to the world. He could score three goals in a game and the expression on his face would never vary. The Fish is close to Malkin in terms of his skill level, but he's at the complete opposite end of the spectrum personality-wise. I wonder what, if anything, we're going to get from The Fish this year.

August 12

Today we flew to Moscow and checked into the Odintsovo Training Centre, which includes a dormitory, a new arena with two ice surfaces, and a great fitness room. We played Khimik Voskresensk in an exhibition game and won 4-3. Khimik is the only other team in the league with a foreign coach, Milos Rziga from the Czech Republic. This is my first overnight stay in Moscow since coming over, and there's a real night-and-day difference from the Moscow I remember. Outside our dormitory are soccer fields, a running track, and a park for citizens with a manmade lake in the middle, a fountain, and lots of benches to sit on. I'm told there are thirty new hockey arenas in Moscow, many with two ice surfaces. They say this is the result of Viacheslav Fetisov's influence as the minister of sport. He will undoubtedly accelerate the development of more Russian players than ever before, given that ice availability has been a limiting factor here for some time now.

August 13

We had a surprise visitor at today's morning skate – Fedor Fedorov, the younger brother of Sergei Fedorov, the Anaheim Mighty Ducks' star. Fedor played for Magnitogorsk for a time during the lockout, and if things don't work out for him in the NHL – he'll attend the

Vancouver Canucks' training camp next month – it may be that he'll play for us. He has great size, speed, and skill, but has not been able to crack an NHL lineup. He's a Fedorov so he has great genes and given a longer look in the NHL he may yet prove he can play at the top level.

Tonight we played Spartak in an exhibition game at their arena. It reminded me of the old Montreal Forum – a hockey shrine with a great mural on the wall and old photos showing important moments in Spartak history, when they won the national championship. Spartak was always the most popular team in Russia in the Soviet days, and may still be. Dynamo was the KGB team, CSKA the army team, and Spartak the workers' team. Up in the rafters there are retired sweaters of such famous players as the Mayorov brothers, Boris and Evgeny, plus Shepelev and Yakushev. Before the game I bumped into David Ling, a Canadian who played a few games for me in Columbus. Playing goal for Spartak was Tyler Moss, a former Calgary Flames' prospect and, like Travis Scott, a solid AHL goalie.

After tying the game 1-1, we bused to the train station and travelled through the night, passing through St. Petersburg before arriving in Lahti, Finland, the next morning, where we'll play in the Tampere Cup, our next-to-last exhibition tournament. The Russians call the Finnish portion of the train trip the "velvet carpet" because the tracks are so much smoother and therefore quieter than on the Russian side of the border.

August 16

Gennady Velichkin, our GM, joined us today, and after meeting with the players he said they complained of being tired and wanted a day off. Instead of two-a-days, we scheduled just a single practice for today – but the execution was so poor that after forty-four practices

I finally blew a fuse. This was actually a calculated blow-up on my part. I wasn't really angry, but I did want to show them my "dark" side – and let them know that I could get plenty steamed if I thought the team was slacking off. Privately, I took Yushkevich and Korolev aside to let them know I did this mainly for show. But I thought it was important for the players to see that a poor effort would get a clear reaction from me.

I like to swim, and there's a lake right across from the training centre where we're staying, so during our time here I'd go down and jump in the lake every morning. It was pretty uneventful – until today. I was swimming down along the shore, about twenty metres out, in front of somebody's cottage, and I could hear a dog barking. Suddenly, I saw this great big German shepherd come wheeling out in the lake, barking and swimming behind me, and I'm thinking, I've never been attacked by a dog in all the years I've been running and now I'm going to be attacked by a dog in the water? What am I going to do? I mean, this thing was gaining on me. I thought, Can a dog bite you in the water? Then suddenly this guy appeared on the dock and yelled at the dog, and finally the dog turned around and headed back. What a relief! I've been chased by elk at the lake and I've had all kinds of other experiences while out exercising, but never anything quite like this.

August 20

We won all three preliminary games in the tournament to qualify for the final, but lost four players to injury along the way. Velichkin was worried because we were down to three lines and had to play with four nineteen-year-olds in the lineup, but I saw it differently. I wanted to know if we could dig down against a good Finnish team like Espoo, and I'm not disappointed by the results. We won 3-2 to win the Tampere Cup and killed off two, two-minute five-on-three power plays. Travis Scott played great and that impressed our management to no end. Malkin got tossed out of the game with a five-minute major late in the first period, so we really needed to stay together as a team and we did. I'm pleased.

August 24

We arrived in Moscow from Lahti, Finland, at eight a.m. following an all-night train trip, but don't fly home until seven p.m. It didn't make a lot of sense to me – but the players were all bused out to the Vnukove airport, where they'll spend the whole day in an airport terminal waiting for our evening flight home. For me, though, it was the best day of summer, because while they were cooling their heels I was off to Sheremetyvo airport to pick up my beautiful wife, who was arriving from Canada today. Linda's spent most of the summer at our cottage in Waskesiu, Saskatchewan, because we knew I'd be immersed in the hockey upon arriving and there'd be little for her to do; it just made sense that she postpone her arrival for as long as possible. But I've missed her terribly. Linda and I were married back in 1970 when I was a student at the University of Saskatchewan and she was working in the accounts office of an Eaton's department store. We have three children: Andy, our oldest son, lives in Calgary with his wife, Sara, and our two adorable grandchildren, Victoria and Daniel; Scott, who lives in Augsburg, Germany, this year with his wife, Katherine; and Jenn, who lives and works in Saskatchewan. I'm not sure if Linda knew the type of vagabond existence she was getting into when she married a hockey coach. It can be a tremendously demanding job – and not just because of the hours you put in at the rink before, during, and after games and practices. There's the travel; there's the videotape work; there's the networking; there are the games to watch. If you want to maintain a semblance of normal family life, it puts a lot of pressure on your spouse – and Linda has done an exceptional job of raising our three kids. The average NHL coach lasts about two-and-a-half years in his job; that was my experience too in Calgary and Columbus. Luckily for us, during the formative years of our kids' lives we had a pretty stable home life because we lived in Calgary from 1983 until 1997 – first, because of my time with the national team, and then because I moved right across town to coach the Calgary Flames. Still, with the national team, we toured the world, and with the Flames, we toured North America. So there were a lot of times when Linda was like a single mother, having to get three kids to all their various activities and with minimal help from me when we were on the road. Since the kids have grown and left the nest, her support of my various ramblings – Japan, Germany, and now Russia – is the only reason I've been able to chase these various dreams of coaching around the world. I know that Barry Smith, when he thought about taking this job, wasn't going to bring his wife over, but when I pitched the idea to Linda she was completely in favour and said that she was coming too. Without that unequivocal vote of confidence, I wouldn't have taken the job.

Linda brought a ton of luggage, mostly full of such North American essentials as Miracle Whip, brown sugar, and other baking products like baking powder, baking soda, and chocolate chips. We jammed her bags into the car and spent the rest of the day shopping while I gave her a rundown of what to expect from Magnitogorsk.

The first thing to know was that there's a night-and-day difference between what we were seeing in Moscow and what she'd see tomorrow on her first day in Magnitogorsk. Moscow is a modern city now, much different from when I used to come here in the 1980s with the national team. There are billboards, advertising, neon signs, just as you'd see in Tokyo or in New York's Times Square. The shopping centres are similar to North America's – with all the same high-end shops. They've spent a lot of money in Moscow, but obviously there's not enough to go around because Magnitogorsk is going to look to Linda the way Moscow once did in the bad old days. Magnitogorsk has only three colours – grey, brown, and black – plus there's the steel mill, which just pumps out smoke, day and night. The city has a low ceiling because of the pollution. Moscow is bright, vibrant, and alive. In time, one can only hope that Magnitogorsk will be the same.

August 25

On Linda's first day in Magnitogorsk, I wanted to take her shopping to see the variety of available food products. The biggest difference between what we had last year in Hamburg and what we're dealing with here is in the quality of the produce – the fruit and vegetables aren't as plentiful and the meat products aren't as abundant. It's also a little disconcerting to be shadowed by the stores' security people, who roam and peek around corners at you as they speak on their walkie-talkies.

Nor am I too keen on the way they just lay out all the beef on the counters in the downtown markets, where we don't shop. It just doesn't look right to me because of the lack of refrigeration. Just before leaving Canada, I got a hepatitis A/B shot. They tell you that within six to eight weeks you need a second shot. So I went to our team doctor when we were in Finland and said: "This is what the vaccine is. Can you get it for me? I know it's available here." He said yes, he could get it. But then Velichkin, our GM, said, "Why are you taking this?" I said, "Our department of health and welfare in Canada recommends that when travelling to Russia you should get a hepatitis A/B shot."

He wasn't annoyed, but a little bit embarrassed. "This is not Africa," he said. "Our health standards are very high in Magnitogorsk." That's their view and that's okay, but it didn't stop me from going ahead and getting my shot anyway.

August 26

The NHL and the International Ice Hockey Federation are currently trying to negotiate a new player transfer agreement, and Velichkin is deeply involved in the talks. He was on the negotiating committee and was really, really intent on coming up with an agreement only if it ensured that existing contracts would be honoured. He was a strong voice in that group – and in the end, the Russian federation was the only one in Europe not to sign the new transfer agreement.

Ironically, today we received the good news that Malkin was indeed going to stay and play out the year. We found out after practice, when the whole team, including players, wives, girlfriends, and kids, were bused up to the MMK-built ski resort in the Ural Mountains, about forty kilometres from here. Malkin took the time to officially inform the press of his decision.

This, of course, came after our organization rewrote and improved his contract and threw in the cost of a *dacha*, a gift from the team. A *dacha* is not unlike our cottages back in Canada; it'd be as if an NHL team like the Toronto Maple Leafs decided to buy a player a cottage on Lake Muskoka to convince him to sign a contract with them. So things have worked out very well for Malkin in this renegotiation, and I suspect they'll work out very well for us too. In Finland, last month at the Tampere Cup, he was just so good. We had a great crowd for our game against Tappara, the local team, and Malkin would do such dazzling things with the puck that the fans just stood up and applauded. That doesn't happen often to a foreign player in a foreign country, but Malkin's artistry was so amazing that they were cheering. I'm hoping to hear that sound over and over again this year.

August 27

It's Saturday, and after the morning training session Linda and I went downtown and walked around city hall, where they were busy grinding out scores and scores of civil weddings at the marriage licence bureau. This was something to see. The cars with the brides and grooms, along with their attendants, were all lined up outside, and in fifteen minutes they were in and out – married and out the door and happily driving around town, horns honking to signify the big day. From there, the happy couples would usually adjourn to the War Memorial, on the banks of the Ural River, or over to the new Russian Orthodox church, to have pictures taken.

There are few churches in Magnitogorsk, given that it was built only in 1929, back when Russia was in the grip of "godless" Communism. So all the churches we've seen are either brand-new or only a few years old. Religion is making something of a comeback here, and one of the most interesting manifestations of that for me is in our dressing room. Pinned up inside virtually every player's locker is a picture of a religious icon. For so many years they couldn't demonstrate or practise their faith, so they're making up for lost time by decorating the walls with these icons. Before stepping on the ice many players also cross themselves in the same way North American athletes have done over the years.

Later, after walking around town, we stumbled across another important find – a pizza place that just opened downtown. A small confession: I'm a pizza junkie, so this is heaven – thin crust and high-quality cheese. It was amazing to find such a thing in this faraway place.

August 28

Goalie Travis Scott's wife, Lisa, and their two kids just arrived last night for a ten-day visit. They're Canadians living in San Antonio; she'll visit two or three times this year, and the team pays for these flights. She'll be coming back in December and he'll go home in November on our ten-day break for national team competition. Every day I make a point of talking to Travis on the ice – and often, it's not about hockey. It's about everything else. We compare notes on what we're seeing and how we're adjusting, and we share stories about how different it all is. For whatever reason, having someone to talk to about those things makes all the difference in the world. Or if I've heard something through the hockey grapevine, I'll say: "Did you hear this is happening in North America?"

The other day we were talking about the hurricane in New Orleans, and he mentioned that he'd played in Baton Rouge for two years and knew some people there. Even Russian TV had quite extensive reports on it, and of course we get CNN in our apartments, so we were able to keep abreast of the story. Travis said he couldn't believe it; he figured the rink must be completely gone because it wasn't a great facility to begin with and was probably full of water.

Now, as anyone involved in hockey can attest, goaltenders tend to be an eccentric breed, presumably because they're putting themselves in the path of a puck that's fired a hundred miles per hour, often at their head. Some goalies are happy-go-lucky, such as Grant Fuhr or Mike Vernon, seemingly without a care in the world. That's how they cope. Others are tightly wound, such as Patrick Roy.

Travis Scott falls more in the second category. He's a serious guy, a little on the quiet side, and you can tell he's a thinker. When I did my homework on him, those were things that worried me a little. Everyone I asked told me that he's a really good guy and a really good teammate, but that he's quiet and does his own thing. I thought, Holy smoke, this could be a problem. Because when trying to add players to our team, the one thing I'm always aware of is how they're going to fit in and whether they can deal with the situation over here. With Travis, I got a mixed review, since other people said, "Oh no, he's mentally a really strong guy." So we had to take a flyer on him. He *is* very quiet. He's very observant. But you can also sense the strength in him. He's got a presence. When he comes on the ice to practise, he's all business.

I know there are times when he's been frustrated. It's not easy for a goaltender to come over here because during practice his teammates might make twenty-seven passes from the top of the circle to the net. I've tried to tell the guys to shoot the puck, but they won't. Sometimes you can hear this loud "Fuuuuuuuck" from the other end of the rink, and without turning around I'll know it'll be Travis – because the players are so creative and artistic that they've basically passed the puck right into the net.

The other thing that's very different for him is all the dryland work we do in our training camp. Our goalie coach is Yuri Shundrov, from Kiev, who works for the Ukrainian federation, and he's got these guys bouncing up and down and over hurdles – things that Travis has never done. Here's an example. We have a game two days from now. This morning we met at ten o'clock and the guys did a thirty-minute warm-up in the gym. Then we went on the ice for an hour and a half. After practice we left the ice and went back upstairs to do forty minutes of fitness – plyometrics and light weights. So Travis is in a totally new environment, since in the American Hockey League you travel so much that you don't get a chance to do any proper off-ice training. I give him a lot of credit because so far he's been pretty resilient. He's passed the test to this point, but it's a major change for him and a major challenge, one that we'll have to keep monitoring.

On the second or third day Linda got here she baked Travis a bag of chocolate chip cookies. He said, "This is great. I'm going to save these for later and have them when I go home to my apartment." He was just thrilled by the gesture; it meant so much because someone was thinking about him.

Linda's been here for a few days now and is slowly adjusting, but even the simplest little tasks can be a chore. Example: we have a Russian bank card, and today Linda phoned me at work in the morning and said, "Dave, I've just gone to two different banks with our bank card and it doesn't work. Do we have any money in the bank?" Yes, we do. I said, "Don't worry, I'll bet that what's happening is the machine is simply out of money." Sure enough, that's what it was. We ended up going to five different bank machines, and they were all empty – because sometimes they don't fill them on the weekends. So if you don't get there on Friday night, often by Saturday afternoon you're out of luck.

August 29

If you watched my team practise or play you'd be impressed by their overall skill level and the number of passes they attempt and complete. However, if you started to analyze it a little deeper – and consider not so much the number of passes but the "value" or advantage gained by the pass – you'd reach the same conclusion as I have. We pass the puck way too much, particularly when we cross the offensive blue line, for no apparent purpose. I'm learning that this is going to be a big part of my coaching challenge: to get our players to get the puck to the net. It's common for us to make so many extra passes that we go from inside to outside the scoring area. As I've stood behind the bench during a game, it's crossed my mind that we're more interested in entertaining than in scoring. We get so cute and so artistic that we become our own worst enemies; eventually, a bad pass will launch our opponent's counterattack and then we're in a poor position to defend because we're too fatigued from entertaining the fans. My hope is that the message slowly sinks in, so that by the time we get to mid-season I'll have weaned the tendency out of our game. I don't expect it to disappear entirely. I'd be happy if it happened even some of the time; that way, we'd be a more unpredictable team and thus more difficult to defend against.

August 30

Working in my office today before practice, I noticed something unusual: the sounds of silence. No music blaring in the dressing room the way it usually does; no sounds of carpentry in the halls, where the players work on their sticks. So I stuck my head out the door and wandered down the hall, right into the middle of a religious service. A Russian Orthodox priest and two cantors were moving around the room, sprinkling holy water on every player as they stood, heads bowed, in front of their locker stalls. Collectively, they were praying for a successful and injury-free season. As I slowly backed into a corner to observe this solemn scene, I couldn't help but think again what an audaciously different experience I was having here in Russia.

August 31

Our final tune-up before the regular season is underway. It's called the Romazan Cup and is a big, big deal here. It's a tournament that we host and that honours the father of hockey in Magnitogorsk: Ivan Romazan, who was president of the steel company before Rashnikov took over. Romazan died of a heart attack at a young age – fifty-five or fifty-six. His picture hangs in the rink; he's revered here for bringing hockey in Magnitogorsk into the twentieth century. As the story goes, after the 1980 Olympics, there was a freeze on building any sports facilities in Russia, because the Olympics had been so expensive. But Romazan convinced Moscow that he was building a cultural facility, a theatre. In reality, what they were building was an indoor ice-hockey stadium. And eventually that allowed them to qualify for the Super League.

All the coaches of all the participating teams went out to Romazan's gravesite. His wife and his daughter were there, and I would say seventy or eighty other people attended as well – a whole busload, plus two vans. We all laid flowers. There were lots of wreaths and everyone held a rose in their hand; one at a time they went forward and put a rose at the base of this huge, huge statue. It's not even a headstone, it's a statue. It was a solemn, solemn ceremony. The profound respect they hold for this man, and for all he did for hockey in Magnitogorsk, was impressive.

September 4

Training camp ended today, and we've had a really good run in the exhibition season. After Yushkevich and Korolev showed up we just took off as a team. Now, suddenly, our practices move along more quickly. Translation has been much more accurate because Igor

Korolev knows how we play in the NHL and some of the things we try to do; as well, his teammates respect him because he's such a senior player. We had our voting for captain today and the players picked Evgeny Varlamov, a twenty-nine-year-old defenceman who's played here for years. Our first assistant is Malkin – and I was quite interested in that; that the players would vote for a nineteen-year-old assistant captain. The other assistant captain is Igor – and that tells you something about how much respect he gets, even though he's been here for only a short period of time.

We didn't lose a game in the first twelve we played in the preseason, and everyone is really happy, but with the regular season just three days away I'm still waiting to see what our team is like. So when we finally lost to Ak Bars Kazan in the second game of our tournament – and lost in a spectacular manner – I was actually relieved. We were up 2-1 and they scored to tie it up with less than three minutes to go. Then they scored again in the final thirty seconds to win 3-2, costing us the game and the tournament. Earlier I'd said to the other coaches, "I hope that somewhere along the line we lose a game, so we can see how well our team bounces back from defeat." In my mind we couldn't get a better script than this. We were leading against a good team, and suddenly we just let it slip away. Everyone was very disappointed. Guys were breaking sticks. I said, "This is the reaction that I hoped we'd get." I'd rather lose that way than 4-1 or 5-1. The next day we had a great game against Moscow Dynamo, the defending league champions, and we won. We finished second in the tournament, which is okay, and we start the regular season next week.

Afterwards I had a chance to talk to the Kazan coach, Zinetula Bilyeletdinov, or coach Bill as he's known throughout the NHL. Bilyeletdinov was a long-time national team player for Viktor Tikhonov and was the longest-serving Russian assistant coach in the NHL – he was with Winnipeg and then with Phoenix before he came home.

Kazan received a lot of international attention during the NHL lockout because they, more than any other team in the world, aggressively recruited locked-out NHL players in a bid to win a championship. It was the thousandth anniversary of the Tatarsan Republic and the oil oligarchs there determined that money would be no object; they'd spare no expense in bringing in the best and the brightest available stars and gambled that the lockout would last the entire NHL season.

They began by signing two members of the Stanley Cup champion Tampa Bay Lightning, Vincent Lecavalier and Brad Richards. When Richards got hurt at Christmas and went home, they replaced him with Dany Heatley. They also signed Atlanta's Ilya Kovalchuk, who had scored forty-one goals in the NHL the previous year, tying him with Jarome Iginla and Rick Nash for the league's goal-scoring title. They had a handful of other prominent Russian players – Alexei Morozov, Darius Kasparaitis, Alexei Kovalev, and from Christmas on, Lecavalier's Tampa teammate, goaltender Nikolai Khabibulin. They were loaded and were soon known throughout the hockey world as Russia's answer to the New York Rangers. Sadly, from their perspective, they also learned the lesson that finally sank in with the Rangers as well – that, in a team game, money doesn't necessarily guarantee a championship. Kazan had a respectable finish in the regular season, but lost in the playoffs.

The other day, Bilyeletdinov signed two Canadian players – Ray Giroux, from New Jersey's farm team, and Jeff Hamilton, a forty-goal scorer in the American Hockey League. They're both really good players and they went to Yale University together, so it was a package deal. They've also got Morozov back this year, as well as Freddie Brathwaite, who played in the NHL for Edmonton and two of my ex-teams, Calgary and Columbus. So they've got their three imports in place now. Freddie played really well against us. We probably could have won that game against Kazan if he hadn't stoned us.

The Russian players told me that before the NHL guys came over, Freddie was the best goalie in the Super League. Then they brought over Khabibulin and started to play him right away, so Freddie got stuck in a backup role. But in the playoffs Khabibulin really stumbled and Freddie came back and played great, even though Kazan underachieved in the playoffs. All the Russian players on Kazan love him. He's very popular. I have a couple of players on my team who played for Kazan last year, and when they saw Freddie they ran right over to him. The funny thing is, he doesn't speak a word of Russian. They speak little English and they love the guy anyway. When he was out of the lineup and not playing he'd stay out on the ice for hours at a time with all the other Russian players who got bumped out of the lineup when the NHL guys arrived. He'd work with them forever, taking shots, and they couldn't believe he'd do that, which is why they came to respect him so much.

So I know coach Bill and I also know one of their players, Gennady Razin, really well. He's a defenceman we had in Montreal when I was an assistant coach with the Canadiens. As a sixth-round choice in the 1997 entry draft, he ended up rooming with my son Scott in Fredericton. They lived together in a house for a year, and now Gennady plays in Kazan. He was saying how difficult it was last year and how much better it is this year.

In fact, everybody I talked to about Kazan said the same thing. Billy told me he had a difficult time coaching last year because with all these superstars coming over there was suddenly a double standard within the team. The NHLers stayed in hotels. They didn't stay in the dormitory, or what's called a *baza* over here, on the night before games. The foreign players hung around together and didn't integrate into the team the way Billy would have liked. Billy even said to me, "I just didn't coach the same way. I had a hard time disciplining these guys, or laying it on the line with them to play harder or to work harder off the ice." But the players I talked to all said that he's a completely different coach now. He's a hard-ass again, like a normal Russian coach. Everybody gets treated exactly the same and things are going that much smoother for them so far this year. I guess we'll see.

Dave has an on-ice chat with fellow Canadian Travis Scott.

Two great warriors. Ex-Leafs Dimitri Yuskevich
and Igor Korolev at practice with Dave.

PART 2 **FALL**

September 5

THERE IS A SEDUCTIVE OPTIMISM TO the start of any new season. No matter how badly things may have gone the year before – or even if things went well – a new season represents a new beginning. Anything and everything seems possible. Hope is palpable, the chance to start fresh intoxicating. The greatest thing about competitive sport is that every year features a handful of unexpected surprise teams and an equal number of bitterly disappointed ones. Sometimes the best teams win, but often they don't, for any number of difficult-to-predict reasons. Intuitively, I know there'll be dog days ahead for our team – times when we're really good and everything will go our way, and times when we're not, and it will seem as if our world is falling apart. We had a good pre-season overall. We won the Tampere Cup. We finished second in the Romazan Cup and second in the Ufa tournament. We should be one of the better teams in the league, but who knows what that will mean once we start playing for points? Sport is unpredictable. That's why they play the games. Slumps can happen and so do injuries, and if you ever lose your starting goaltender for any length of time, you can be in trouble.

Of course, there's a difference between hope and expectation. I coached two teams in the NHL – Calgary and Columbus. With the Flames in '94, my expectations were quite high. I thought we'd be one of the top teams in our division, and that if everything went well we should be a contending team all the way. By contrast, when

I took over the Blue Jackets, we were a first-year expansion team. You still find yourself full of hope, but your expectations are different. You hope to overachieve, and if you do, you consider that a successful year, even if you missed the playoffs.

In the NHL the optimism builds throughout the summer, usually starting with the entry draft in June. No matter who you draft, you always hear the same refrain from the scouts: "We can't believe this guy was available at our pick." Even down in the tenth round, you hear them say, "Holy cow! How did this guy last this long!" And as the summer moves along, all your players just keep getting better and better in your own mind – when they aren't playing. For some reason we also automatically assume that any player who had an off-season the year before is going to bounce back in a big way. Conversely, if a guy had a great season, you don't worry that he might not be able to do it again. You just figure it'll happen. So you really go into a new season thinking nothing but positive thoughts and it feels great – until reality catches up to you, as it almost certainly will.

Now, my situation – coming to Russia – was far different from any other previous experience because I didn't know the team. I knew they had some good players. I saw Malkin play at the world championships and knew he was an excellent talent. Magnitogorsk finished fifth last year and won the championship about five years ago, so I knew I was going to a fairly stable organization. But until training camp started two months ago, I'd never seen them play. So while I find myself generally optimistic, I'm also more uncertain than usual because I don't know the league, I don't know my team, I don't know my players, and I don't know if my approach is going to work. There are a lot of Super League teams I haven't seen yet, and playing for points generally promotes greater intensity in the competition. Anticipation is what I'm feeling today, along with a little anxiety, excitement, and nervousness thrown in for good measure.

Now, just about any player who's ever played for me will tell you

I'm a stickler for detail. I believe in preparation and conditioning, in video work and in reviewing tactics and tendencies, so that when you go out onto the ice you're ready on every level to play the game. But even I have found the past two months of preparation to be excessively long. The players were obviously readier for this than I was. In hindsight, I can see why they came to camp in less than ideal condition. They understood that they had two months to find their stride. I think they're ready.

Our season opener is in two days' time against Vityaz, one of the two new teams in the league. As a result of this latest expansion, there's a new playoff format in the Super League. Last year, in a sixteen-team league, eight qualified for the playoffs. This year, in an eighteen-team league, sixteen qualify for the playoffs, so obviously, the higher you finish, the easier your playoff path will be. The Russian schedule lasts fifty-one games and is divided into three distinct seventeen-game rounds. In the first round, you play every team once. In the second round, you play them again in reverse order. We don't have the schedule yet for the third round – it'll be determined by the league standings after thirty-four games. The top nine teams all get an extra home date and the schedule will be weighted in favour of the teams that had success in the first two-thirds of the season. I like the way that works, but I can't imagine that a concept such as this would ever fly in the NHL. Can you imagine telling your season-ticket holders that they won't know what the final third of the schedule will look like until it's actually upon them? I couldn't either.

But then, there are a lot of things they do differently here. Russia, for example, operates the same way as the rest of Europe does in terms of transferring players from one team to another. There are virtually no trades per se, the way we're used to in the NHL. Instead, during the two predetermined breaks in the schedule, teams can modify or adjust their rosters, usually by signing players from another league or by selling players into the marketplace. Because salaries have gone up in Russia, teams can reasonably look at possible NHL castoffs as recruits for down the road. The problem, of course, is that NHL training camps haven't even opened yet; it'll be a month before they complete their final cuts.

Once that happens, a number of teams, including ours, will be looking to see which players don't make an NHL roster so that we can potentially bid on their services. Right now we have just the one import, Travis Scott. We left the other two import cards open. I like the way our team looks now and I'm prepared to go with this group, at least until the first transfer window opens in November. At that point we can look at what we need, and at what players might be available, and then make a decision. Also, there is no way of forecasting what injuries we might have in the months ahead, so my vote was to stay with the status quo, keep those import cards open, and re-evaluate at the first break in the schedule. As it is, we have a twenty-five-man roster, and even accounting for our injured players, we still have extras.

Tomorrow, owner and team president Rashnikov will address our team, something he apparently does every year just before the start of the regular season. I haven't spoken to him since our first meeting back in early July, so I'm interested in hearing what he has to say. Sometimes, in the NHL, an owner will want to stop by and talk to the team, either as a group, or after a game when he's with friends and family interested in meeting a "star" player. Somehow, based on the little I know of the man, I suspect the Rashnikov meeting will unfold quite differently.

September 6

I'm fascinated by Rashnikov because I've heard and read so much about the Russian oligarchs and I can't seem to get a straight answer about his rise to power in the post-Soviet era – or how he accumulated so much wealth so quickly. As promised, he came in and spoke to our team the night before our first game in the arena's player dining area. He showed up with two bodyguards. Both wore earplugs, just as if they were part of the U.S. Secret Service. They were big, big men. One stationed himself by the door at the back of the restaurant. The other covered the door in the front. I was thinking, Holy mackerel, this guy's worth so much money, I guess he needs to do this all the time. I've been told that the biggest crime in Russia isn't bank robbery or anything like that, it's kidnapping. As a result, Viktor Rashnikov has become a very, very careful man.

His message to our players was straightforward, and was the same one he delivered to me at our first meeting eight weeks ago – that nothing less than playing in the Super League semifinal will be good enough. He explained to the players that the MMK Steel Company invests millions of dollars in the team, and the results are important in terms of how they market the company. The employees follow the team closely and take pride in their successes – and there've been a lot of those in the recent past. Twice, they won the Super League crown. They also won the European Champions League twice. For a small city of less than half a million, the hockey team puts it on the map.

After our supper meeting with Rashnikov, the players all caught the team bus to our *baza*. The *baza* is a tradition in Russian ice hockey that dates back to the Communist era, when the players would be segregated from their families for long portions of the schedule. Generally, a *baza* is a team-owned dormitory where the players sleep the night before a home game so that they can prepare themselves without the distraction of family, friends, or just the day-to-day demands of life. In the old days of communal living, the athletes lived in apartments but shared the common areas – kitchens and bathrooms – so a player couldn't necessarily get the peace and quiet he needed to prepare for a game. The teams here want the players to focus squarely on hockey, and they believe that putting them in the *baza* the night before a game helps accomplish that. In my view, it may well work just the opposite way. We spend so much time together on the road anyway that forcing the players to go to the *baza* when they're at home becomes counterproductive because it keeps them apart from their families.

The other complicating factor is that MMK is in the process of building not only a new arena but a new *baza* as well, and because of the construction we don't actually have an on-site *baza* any more. The plan is to use a local hotel as a *baza* until the new complex is complete. When I heard this, I innocently suggested that maybe we could do without the *baza* for a year. Well, that idea was shot down instantly. It was as if I'd uttered something sacrilegious. They told me, "We have to have the *baza*. We always have the *baza*." I said, "Gee, a lot of guys don't like it because they spend six out of every seven days in a hotel or a *baza*, so if their families are here with them, they never get to see them." But no, we had to have the *baza*, so tonight we went to the *baza*. This sort of thinking continues to amaze me. In the new Russia these guys all drive BMWs into the parking lot, but when they go into the rink it's all old-school again, right down to the need to stay in a *baza*. It's a real contrast.

September 7

It's a beautiful sunny day – Labour Day weekend back home – and hardly hockey weather at all. On my morning walk to the arena I can see the MMK steel factory operating at full capacity on my left, and it struck me that our arena operates in much the same fashion. It's virtually a hockey factory, busy from eight o'clock in the morning until eleven o'clock at night. Every day, both ice surfaces are used to capacity. This morning there were some eleven- and twelve-year-olds training as I entered the arena, so I stopped to watch them for a few minutes. I found the level of concentration high and the tempo fast. As I walked past the players' bench the coach stopped practice and gathered all the players at the bench area, where they greeted me with a chorus of "*Oodachee*," meaning good luck. I was feeling the buzz and the adrenalin flow early on; I'd even quickened the tempo of my morning run to get myself energized. After all the pomp and ceremony associated with the Romazan Cup I wanted to know what they had in mind for opening night, so I arrived at my office well before anyone else to review our training sessions and our game lineup without any interruptions.

After our pre-game skate ended, Igor Korolev and Dmitri Yushkevich skated over and told me that our temporary *baza*, a small hotel outside of Magnitogorsk, had been a disaster the previous night. The beds were small and saggy. The hotel bar was open until two a.m. and people came by knocking on our players' hotel-room doors, asking if they wanted to party. As well, a few of the players had mice visit their rooms. Needless to say, our management was angry and promised the players that we'd switch hotels for the next game. I'm anxious to see if our players can park this problem and be ready to play, because the assumption is that we're going to win tonight's game quite easily.

Just before the puck drop, as I was standing behind the bench and listening to the Russian national anthem, I looked across the rink and found Linda in the stands, getting ready to cheer us on, and suddenly the whole situation just seemed so unreal to me. Here I was, about to become officially the first Canadian to coach in the Russian Super League, and I still wasn't used to the idea. The first little while over here was a huge transition for me. Every day I kept asking myself, Can you fit in here? Can you adjust? I was about to find out.

As it turned out, our start was terrible. Vityaz scored the first goal – from Alexander Korolyuk, the ex-San Jose Shark player. We got into penalty trouble early and gave them the lead, but eventually our guys got more disciplined and we started to wear them down. In the end, we won comfortably 6-2. Truthfully, I was more relieved than happy. I just wanted to get it over with, to get a game that counted for points in the standings under our collective belts. At the post-game press conference I was peppered with questions about the experience of being the first Canadian coach in Russia. I kept my replies simple and brief. I explained that it is an honour to coach in Russia and that Linda and I were looking forward to a wonderful adventure – which was exactly how I felt.

After the game, the tradition in Russia is for the coach and his wife to go into the VIP lounge and socialize with the management for a time. My usual practice is to go straight home and break down the game tape, but this tradition predates my presence here and it's clearly important to them, so I went with the flow. That was a good thing because it gave us a chance to digest the other first-day action around the league. It turned out that the defending champions, Moscow Dynamo, weren't as fortunate as we'd been. They got beat, in overtime, at home by MVD, one of the new teams in the league. That was an emotional day all over the league because it was also the day that Dynamo and Avangard Omsk, the Roman Abramovich team, reportedly settled their tug-of-war over the services of Pavel Datsyuk.

Datsyuk, the Detroit Red Wings' young star, played for Dynamo during the NHL lockout, but he signed a new contract in the off-season with Omsk. Datsyuk had been practising and training with Omsk all through August and September; he'd basically said no to his NHL team, and this was big, big news here because, for the first time ever, a Russian team had outbid an NHL team for a player. Or so it seemed at the time.

Dynamo announced that they had matched Omsk's contract offer and argued that that gave them the right to retain his services. Either way, Datsyuk was set to earn a little over $4 million (and

$4 million in the Super League is equivalent to about $6 million in the NHL because of favourable tax laws over here). Datsyuk was a really important guy in Dynamo's success in the lockout year. I watched videotape of him in the playoffs and he single-handedly won games for them. He was probably the best player in the league last year, and that included all the NHL imports. So when our guys heard that Datsyuk was getting $4 million, they were flabbergasted by his salary. It was total silence when they heard the news. I asked, "What do you think?" They all said: "Oh, this is bad. We can't have this in the Russian Super League."

That, I think, was one of the myths that the NHL lockout promoted – that there's unlimited money in Russia nowadays. Yes, there was unlimited money in Kazan last year, and Omsk doesn't look as if it's backing off from recruiting and paying players either, but they appear to be the exceptions. There are small- and medium-market teams in Russia, just as there are in the NHL. I would characterize us as a medium-market team. Our budget is about $21 million. So for us to invest $4 million in one player would mean committing close to a fifth of our budget to one guy. That's just too rich for our blood. We've got a reasonable budget to work with, but we're not one of the big spenders either. Kazan, Omsk, and Dynamo – those teams appear to have more money than anybody else and they also spend more money than anybody else. We're somewhere between sixth and eighth in terms of payroll this season. That's a reasonable amount, and if you spend it wisely it's more than adequate to ice a winning team. Just like in the NHL, it's not how much you spend. It's how you spend it.

One of the things that consistently puzzle me is the lack of homework they do on players here compared with the NHL. We signed two players from Lada after last season. One of them, Alexander Seluyanov, came to us with a back injury we didn't know about. So he got here, went through training camp, and suddenly he was hurt and we had to take him to Chelyabinsk so that he could have a disc operated on. Our management had no idea that was coming. His defence partner, Vladimir Malenkikh, had a leg injury they thought was going to be fine, but when he got here for training camp he couldn't skate for the first month.

I'll tell you, the old guys, like Punch Imlach and Eddie Shore, would have had a great time in Russia – they'd be trading guys with one leg and getting away with it. There's a real demand for the good players. If you're even just a reasonable player, you'll have eighteen teams looking at you. That's a lot of teams. I asked our management: "How can you sign these two players, if one has a back problem and you knew the other guy was hurt because he missed the last twenty games, but you weren't aware that he couldn't skate for the first month?" Their answer was simple: "It's a competitive marketplace." They knew that both players had some problems, but the competition for their services was hot and heavy. That's how they justified the moves. It's an interesting way of doing business, and so different from what I'm used to.

Another thing: we don't rate other teams' players. In the NHL everyone has a book on every player in the league, so if you're looking at making a move, you can consult your own internal scouting database to get a good picture of the player's strengths and weaknesses. I don't know whether to suggest we do that or not – whether we want to be the first team to have a rating system. Given the limited movement from team to team once the season gets underway, it may not be worth the effort.

September 9

We beat MVD, another of the new teams, 5-0 with Travis Scott getting the shutout in his Super League debut. We now go on the road to play Khimik Voskresensk and Avangard Omsk, two teams picked to finish high in the standings after having excellent pre-season results. Khimik will give me a chance to watch Ilya Kovalchuk play first-hand. Like Datsyuk, Kovalchuk is using the threat of playing in the Super League as leverage in his contract talks with the Atlanta Thrashers. Datsyuk didn't play on opening night because of the uncertainty over his status, but Kovalchuk did suit up for Khimik. Unlike Datsyuk, who did train with Omsk, Kovalchuk hadn't even been skating. He played the opener for Khimik and it was only his second or third time on skates in three months. They lost and he didn't play very well. Russian newspapers say that Atlanta will come back with one more substantial offer, and the betting here is that Kovalchuk will return to the NHL – because Khimik certainly doesn't have the money to pay him what Atlanta can. Andrei Nikolishin ended up signing with Lada for about $900,000, so it looks as if he's staying in Russia after ten years in the NHL.

There is a real uncertainty now in terms of players coming and going between the Super League and the NHL because there's no transfer agreement in place between the two organizations. About the only sure thing – and the one thing everybody can agree on – is that if a Russian plays a single Super League game after the NHL season opens on October 5, he basically can't go to the NHL this year. It looks more and more as if Datsyuk is fed up with the tug-of-war between Omsk and Dynamo for his services and he might just opt to play for the Red Wings after all. Kovalchuk, though, is staying put – for now.

September 12

At the pre-game skate in Voskresensk I ran into my old coaching colleague Vladimir Vasiliev, who coached Khimik for years. Vasiliev's coaching mentor was Nikolai Epstein, who died just a few days ago. Epstein was the godfather of Voskresensk hockey and trained such stars as Igor Larionov, Valeri Kamensky, and German Titov. He's little known outside of Russia, but internally he's revered alongside Anatoli Tarasov and others who made such great contributions to Russian hockey.

Most Canadians started paying attention to Russian hockey after the '72 Summit Series, but not much is known about their program between that time and 1956, when they first appeared on the international scene by unexpectedly winning the Olympic gold medal. In that sixteen-year period, the general feeling in Canada was that the Russians were competitive within the context of playing against our "amateurs" and senior players and the national teams that Father David Bauer put together, but that they were nowhere near the same level as our top NHL professionals. That myth was exposed in '72, but obviously their development into a hockey power didn't happen overnight. And it evolved during a time when Tarasov and his colleagues were at the controls. They basically started Russian hockey.

I knew Tarasov, and I knew he was greatly influenced by the training philosophies of a Canadian named Lloyd Percival, but mostly the Russians borrowed liberally from the Czechs and the way their game evolved. The Czechs were playing hockey in the 1920s and 1930s, so they had a tradition that the Russians never had. But the Russians really studied the game; they trained and played for a couple of years internally before they started to compete internationally. Their emergence was just so sudden – they jumped in and within two years won their first world championship. It shocked everybody. Everyone asked: "Who are these guys? How can they do this?" Plus, their style of play was so different from what we were used to. The Swedes and the Finns of that era played more of a Canadian game. The Russians, as well as borrowing some things from the Czechs, brought in tactics from basketball, soccer, and bandy. They interchanged positions. The back passes and the drop passes and all that weaving confused the heck out of everybody.

And all these guys – Tarasov, Vasiliev, and Epstein – were responsible for it all, which is why there was a moment of silence to honour Epstein's memory before the game. From there we went out and played a tough game against Khimik that ended in a 2-2 tie, an okay result under the circumstances.

September 14

After practice today in Voskresensk, we took a charter flight to Omsk, a city of about a million people on the Siberian plain. Omsk is gorgeous and not at all stark or barren the way you might think, with more trees than anywhere else in Russia. The arena looks like a pyramid from the outside, which makes the interior really unusual. There should be room for ten thousand seats, but because of its unique shape it seats only fifty-five hundred. The owner, Roman Abramovich, is the oligarch who also owns the Chelsea soccer team, and he's announced plans to build a new $90 million arena. Omsk is where Jaromir Jagr and other NHL stars played during the lockout, on a team that had a budget of between US$60 and $70 million. We lost the game 4-1 and played poorly. Simchuk, our Russian-Ukrainian goalie, struggled, and we didn't give him a lot of help. The flight home was quiet; the players all knew they hadn't done enough to win.

September 15

Just before practice, both Velichkin and Kuprianov, our GM and assistant GM, came into my office and I sensed right away that they were in a panic mode after the loss to Omsk. They wondered if the assistant coaches shouldn't do more of the motivation and if I should focus on the tactics and preparation. Rashnikov, our owner, was apparently disappointed by our game against Omsk and voiced his displeasure. I assured them both that I didn't expect us to go undefeated and that often an embarrassing loss isn't a bad way to drive home a few important teaching points. I was able to calm them down and told them that we had to give our team a chance to deal with some adversity so that they could grow as a group. I also reminded them that we had some of the best pre-season results of all the Super League teams and that, given time, my approach and the team's character would work out just fine.

The problem, as I gathered, was that last year Magnitogorsk really struggled against the big-name teams, such as Omsk, which was why our loss the other day was suddenly such a big deal. One of the questions I asked myself before I even took the job was, Why did they want to bring in a Canadian as a coach anyway? Last year the coach here was a Czech, Marek Sykora, the father of Petr Sykora, who's back playing in the NHL again this year. In Marek Sykora's first year behind the bench the team finished third and everybody was pretty happy. Last year they finished fourth, got knocked out in the second round of the playoffs, and everybody was quite unhappy. They track an unbelievable number of stats here, and Sykora's downfall as a coach was that his teams fared so poorly against top-level competition. They determined that in games against the league's top eight teams, Magnitogorsk finished seventh. Where they made up ground was beating up on the league's bottom feeders. So while they acknowledged that last year's team got a lot of points, and yes, they finished fourth, and yes, they made it to the second round of the playoffs, they were still disappointed because they hadn't done well against the teams Rashnikov really wants to beat. In the playoffs they won the first two games of a best-of-five against Omsk, but then lost the next three to lose the series. That was the kiss of death for Marek Sykora. I can see it might be the kiss of death for me too, if we can't get that trend reversed.

September 20

Anders Hedberg, the Ottawa Senators' director of player personnel, called today to ask questions about Alexei Kaigorodov, our slick young centre whom they drafted in the second round back in 2002. NHL teams are now about a week into training camp and are pondering the implications of a new set of rules that were introduced after the lockout was settled and are intended to make the game more offensively oriented. The Senators were thinking that if there was indeed going to be more open ice and less obstruction in the game, Kaigorodov was suddenly a more attractive commodity – and he did finish second in the Super League last season in scoring. Kaigorodov has great acceleration and is an absolutely pinpoint passer. His vision makes him a classic Larionov-type playmaker. On our team he plays mostly with Stanislav Chistov, who played briefly for the Anaheim Mighty Ducks during their run to the 2003 Stanley Cup final. They were a dynamic duo on the Russian national junior team for a couple of years there as well. They've always played together, so they share a real bond.

Chistov is small and he's playing with us, as opposed to the NHL, because he can make better money here than if he were playing in the minors for Anaheim. We signed him before the lockout ended and I wondered if he might be interested in going back after the NHL settled the labour dispute, but he told me no, he was staying. He really wants to make the Russian Olympic hockey team and thinks his chances will be enhanced if he plays under the nose of the national team coach all season long. Chistov played for a defensive-oriented coach in Mike Babcock, so he knows a little bit about defensive-zone coverage.

We're spending a lot of time working with Kaigorodov on video and on drills to improve his defensive play low in the defensive zone. Although he's a decent "contain"-type checker, he needs to get a more physical edge to his defensive game. But he's a very professional young man, who works hard in practice and wants to get better. He told me that his dream is to play in the NHL. I suspect he'll see that dream come true one day.

September 21

In all the years I travelled regularly to Russia, one of the great adventures was flying Aeroflot, the national airline, with its decrepit equipment, its mediocre service, and the sometimes genuine fear that you might not make it down in one piece. Today we took a charter flight to Nizhnekamsk and the old fears bubbled up again. Up to this point, with the exception of all those five a.m. arrivals in Magnitogorsk, our travel hasn't been bad. The charter craft have, for the most part, featured modern, up-to-date planes, but today we're in a time warp, flying on a twin-propeller plane the players call Pterodactyl Air – for reasons that are self-explanatory. I'm sure the plane was built in the 1950s. The seats are small and flimsy. The luggage compartment is so tiny we have to stack the hockey bags in the first four rows of seats. Plus, it doesn't seem as if the normal flight rules apply here, at least not when we're chartering. Today, for example, as we took off, the seats were *not* in the full upright position. Tray tables were *down*. The players had their computers and iPods going, and the luggage was certainly not stored properly. The crew would disappear for long stretches to the back of the aircraft, and even though it's supposed to be non-smoking you can catch a whiff of cigarette smoke any time you venture towards the restrooms.

As for the dress code, well, there just isn't one. At one end of the scale is someone like Nikolai Kulemin, who takes a lot of pride in his appearance. Kulemin, like Malkin, is just nineteen and generally wears a nice sweatsuit, the way European athletes usually do. He looks like a tennis star in a lot of ways. At the other end of the spectrum is Stanislav Chistov, or Cheesy, as we call him. Maybe it's because of that year he spent in Anaheim, but he looks like an American skateboarder. His jeans are baggy; the crotch hangs down almost to knee level. His jeans look as if someone ran a lawnmower over them. His jacket has an English-language inscription on the back, but the words make no sense. He wears a variety of new-old running shoes and oddball hats that draw attention to him wherever he happens to be. In some ways, the way they dress is also indicative of how they play. Kulemin is disciplined, efficient, and consistent. Chistov likes to gamble and to freelance. He plays much more on instinct than on plan. If you saw us pass through an airport you'd be more likely to think we were roadies for a rock band than a professional hockey team.

September 22

I had a great run today in Nizhnekamsk, in a beautiful park close to our hotel. On my run I saw my first McDonald's restaurant outside of Moscow. I'm dumbfounded that in a city of only 250,000 they have a McDonald's. Our game is at six p.m., so I make plans for a visit; after weeks of eating in our cafeteria, a hamburger sounds great.

Later, I watched the Neftekhimik pre-game skate and noticed that their coach used a microphone to shout instructions during the drills. Anyone who's ever coached can tell you that one of the greatest concerns is actually being heard by the entire group of players, especially if they're not grouped around you in a cluster by the chalkboard. I've never seen this technique before, but it might be worth looking into.

We won 5-4 in overtime and made a great comeback after being down 4-1. The dressing room was really alive, thanks to this character win. Simchuk struggled in goal, and now I'm sure we should give the net to Travis Scott and let him play until he shows signs of fatigue.

September 23

We're still flying Pterodactyl Air, this time into Kazan, for the first time this year. Most people who followed hockey during the NHL lockout have probably heard of Kazan, because they recruited a star-studded lineup of players. Given that some NHL players had a hard time adjusting to life in this faraway place, I was curious to see what the city looks like.

In some ways it reminded me of St. Petersburg with its architecture and bridges. The city is a thousand years old, but a lot of new building is going on and what isn't new is nicely renovated. Within the walls of the Kremlin lies a new Muslim mosque that's the largest in Europe. And their new 10,500-seat arena, part of the Super League building boom, is just about completed and will open in December.

September 24

Tonight we won 3-1 and played one of our smartest games so far. A victory over Kazan, a team that's battling us for first place, should relieve some of the pressure on me and convince Velichkin that we're on the right track. Just before the game I spoke with Fred Brathwaite again. Even this early in the season, he says it might be his last year in Russia. The money is so good that it's a strong lure, especially for someone who'd be borderline to play regularly in the NHL at this stage of his career. And Kazan is a fascinating place, but a lot of things about the day-to-day life over here can really grind you down.

September 29

Malkin missed practice yesterday after hurting his shoulder in a 3-1 win over Spartak, but it doesn't sound like a serious injury. At our video review session we stressed one point to our players – they should spend more time trying to impress the coaches than the fans.

I watched the Lokomotiv Yaroslav practice and then talked briefly with Vladimir Yurzinov, their coach. Yurzinov was Tikhonov's assistant coach during my nine-year tenure with Canada's national team, so I know him well. He's an accomplished career coach, and when he coached in TPS Turku, Finland, he changed the direction of Finnish hockey. He proved to all the Finnish coaches that their players could withstand a much greater volume of training than the Finns had ever done. He worked his players in the typical Russian model and they won, so other coaches started to follow his training style and soon Finnish hockey was on the rise.

We won 3-0 over Lokomotiv Yaroslav and played our best game of the season so far.

September 30

I'm enjoying our home-ice winning streak because it's taking some of the pressure off me. Velichkin, I'm learning, is something of a worrywart. He's obsessed with the Internet, which is how he gets most of his feedback from fans. There's no sports talk radio in Magnitogorsk, but our website is well done and includes a question-and-answer feature where fans can express their thoughts on our progress. Velichkin monitors their posts religiously, and it appears to affect his decision-making. I can't imagine that any hockey executive in North America would be swayed by popular opinion, except in the rarest of cases.

I usually spend more time dealing with the press, and overall they've been very easy to work with. They're polite; they don't ask many prying questions. They'll report what you say. They're not looking to make a big splash. But sometimes, just when you start to think they're docile and that you have them under control, they'll throw a statistic at you that makes you realize they do their homework. They know what's going on. They don't write much that's negative, but they keep you alert. So the coach-media thing has been very easy.

October 2

We're in Perm to play Molot, one of the league's bottom dwellers. They're in the news, not so much for they're doing on the ice, but for what's happening to them off the ice. According to newspaper accounts, about three weeks ago one of their senior executives flew to Cypress for a holiday with U$450,000 and failed to purchase a return flight. The players haven't been paid since the start of the season and they run their program on a shoestring anyway, so this news is practically catastrophic for a team that struggles annually just to stay in the top league.

We won 4-0 and played a very solid game. Afterwards I took my interpreter, Igor, uptown for a pizza. As we walked along a city bus stopped in the middle of the road and the driver jumped out, sprinted over to me on the sidewalk, and requested my autograph with everyone on the bus staring intently, wondering who I was and what was going on. That was a first for me.

October 4

In Moscow to play the fabled Central Red Army team, we're staying at a hotel just outside the gates of the Red Army sports centre. I was about to head into the sports shop in the arena with Igor to see what they sell in a typical souvenir shop when a well-dressed gentleman stopped me and introduced himself. It was Viacheslav Anisin. I said, "'72?" – and right away, up goes his hand and there's the ring from the famed Summit Series against Canada, that wonderful, historic eight-game competition that gave Russian hockey instant credibility on the world stage. Anisin spoke enough English to say, "Yes, that's me, '72." If you look back at the '72 films, he was the bright young star of that team – he and Lebedev – they were twenty years old, playing for the national team, and he was very proud of that accomplishment. Foster Hewitt had a lot of fun with his name, suggesting that he and his linemates created a lot of "headaches" for the Canadian team. His son is an excellent player too – he plays for the Red Army youth team for fifteen- and sixteen-year-olds, and is apparently going to be a really good player.

So many of these players from the '72 team are struggling with their health and with their pensions, but Anisin was clearly an exception. He was smartly dressed. He looked as fit as a fiddle, as if he hadn't gained a pound. You could almost tell by looking at his face that he was a guy who liked to do things athletically. Some of the others from that team, like Maltsev, look so old now. In Spartak the other day, Yuri Liapikin came over and wanted to talk to me. I'd met him once before in Japan when he and I were both coaching there. Of course, he flashed a '72 ring at me as well. But when you see Liapikin, you see someone with lots of miles on him.

There are more than a dozen banners at one end of the CSKA arena, featuring the retired numbers of some of their most famous players. Curiously, some of these numbers have been retired more than once. There's Firsov, Petrov, Tretiak, Ragulin, Fetisov, and others, but so far, no Krutov or Makarov, which is odd considering that both won the Golden Stick as the top player in Russia and both were on multiple Olympic and world championship-winning teams. The Red Army training centre is only one subway stop up from the Dynamo sports centre, which obviously enhances the rivalry.

After a great stretch of wins, we finally played a poor game and lost 4-3 to end the road trip on a sour note.

October 5

Later today, half a world away, the NHL season starts with fifteen regular-season games, and this has great implications for our league. Datsyuk left for the NHL about two weeks ago, signing a contract with Detroit that will pay him far less than what he would have made had he stayed here. Kovalchuk is technically still on the Khimik roster, but they've announced that he'll leave next week to go to New York so that he can visit his girlfriend, who has just given birth to their daughter. If Kovalchuk were to play a game in the Super League after today, he wouldn't be allowed to play in the NHL this season. Publicly, he keeps insisting that Russia is a viable alternative if Atlanta doesn't give him the contract he wants, but no one here thinks he'll be back. He'll use the threat of playing in Russia as leverage, but when the negotiations come to a head, he'll opt to stay in Atlanta.

October 6

In talking with Igor Korolev today, I learned something new: how he ended up playing for Moscow Dynamo as opposed to Red Army when he was a youngster. Igor lived in a suburb of Moscow, about forty-five minutes outside of town. In those days, the really good kids were all scouted by the Moscow-based teams and encouraged to come to their tryout camps when they were about ten years old. One hundred kids might show up for these tryouts, and that number would eventually be pared down to about twenty-five. I thought Dynamo might have made a big sales pitch to get him, but no, it was much simpler than that. Because he was so young, his parents took him to practice the first couple of times. The Dynamo sports centre was one subway stop closer to their home than the Red Army's. So that was one advantage. The second advantage was that if he went to Red Army he'd have to get off the train with his equipment bag and his stick and cross Leningradsky Prospekt, one of the busiest streets in Moscow. So his mother said, "You're going to go to Dynamo because it's safer for you to travel there."

In those days the vast majority of the best players in Russia ended up playing for Viktor Tikhonov on the Central Red Army team. The exceptions were the other Moscow-based teams: Dynamo, which was the secret police or KGB team; the Soviet Wings, the air force team; and Spartak, the people's or workers' team. There was an informal understanding among those four teams not to touch one another's players. Red Army could get their hands on players from outside of Moscow only by conscripting them. So, for example, with someone like Igor Larionov, who grew up in Voskresensk, as soon as he turned a certain age and was drafted into the Army, Tikhonov's team could grab him, even if he didn't want to go. Most of the Red Army players were developed internally in their own sports club, but they also drafted players from the outlying areas that often made the difference between winning and losing.

Korolev is happy playing with us, but if it were up to him, I think he'd still be playing for the Maple Leafs in Toronto this season. I continue to be impressed with both him and Yushkevich. They're old warhorses and have a lot of miles on them, but they're effective players for us. I'm not sure how our management feels about the decision to sign them, though. Presumably, if they physically hold up for the entire season and help us win, it'll make management re-evaluate their attitude to older players. Yushkevich's legs are heavier than they ever were before, but he gets by on his head and his competitiveness and his conditioning. He's in mint, mint condition, except for that left leg, which is just really bad. But he's played every game for us and hasn't missed a practice either.

The other day Yushkevich blocked a shot and got hit in the face doing it. We got a breakaway off the shot and scored the winning goal. That's the kind of player he is. He's lying at the ice, at one end, bleeding. The referee looks at him, doesn't think it's a serious injury, lets the play go on, and we score on the rush. I put it on the videotape because it was a heck of a shot block. My god! His timing was poor, but he went right down and blocked it with his face. I didn't think I'd see him for a while, but the next day, who's there at practice? It's Yushkevich – and he looked like hell. If little kids on the street had seen him they would have run the other way. He looked like a character in a horror movie, with all those scars of his and now his face all lopsided. He's amazing. He's a little like a Scott Stevens type. He loves to play and loves to practise.

He's been back in Russia for three years now, and deep down I believe he'd still like one more crack at the NHL. In his last year in the NHL he played for three different teams – Florida, Los Angeles, and Philadelphia – and I think the word got out that, for all his competitiveness, he's a one-legged player now, which may be easier to hide in this league than in the NHL.

Yushkevich played in Yaroslav two years ago, for Cherepovets during the lockout, and now he's with us. We were talking about the changes he's seen in his career the other day and he told me, "The game over here has changed a great deal in terms of marketing. There are cheerleaders, and new arenas going up. All these cosmetic things are new and different, but the fundamental core of the game for the players is exactly the same." He added, "You don't yell, but all the other coaches in the league yell and scream at their players just like they did before. They treat you like shit and they work the hell out of you. Nothing has changed that way. We get paid a lot more money than we did before but we're still treated the same way." Interesting – in the NHL, I'm a hard-ass. In Russia, suddenly I'm a moderate.

October 10

One of the Viktors – Suchov, my second assistant – turned fifty today, so there was a party and everyone was expected to toast the birthday boy. So I did – in broken Russian, to the best of my ability. I'm thinking more and more about what Yushkevich said about Russian coaches and how they treat their players. He believes the players expect that sort of harsh treatment and just shrug it off – that over the years, they learn to be resilient and develop a thick skin, since it's still common to see an unrelenting coach berating a player on the bench.

I believe in being direct and firm, but rarely do I percolate to the point of an eruption. In fact, only twice in my NHL career did I erupt on the bench with a player, once with Igor Ulanov and once with Sergei Makarov, both Russians. Believe me, the irony is not lost on me. As a coach, I try to make sure that besides telling the players what to do I tell them why we do it, on the grounds that they'll execute better if they understand the thinking behind the tactics and the system. And in coaching, any time you rely on a translator, you should be aware that a picture (that is, a video clip) is worth a thousand words. When Korolev provides the translation for our video sessions, the feedback I get from the players is that the message is coming through loud and clear. For obvious reasons, that's pivotal in what I'm trying to do here.

One of the biggest adjustments for any coach working in Europe (and this happened to me in Germany too) is how little input you have into the composition of your staff. In the NHL, or with the Canadian national program, you handpick your staff in the same way that you select your team – finding coaches with a particular area of expertise, so that collectively you have all the important areas covered: tactics, video preparation, player liaison, and so on. Our staff here consists of six coaches, which is far more than I'm used to. The hardest part of a large staff is making everyone feel as if they're making a contribution. I've delegated one meaningful job to each coach, but I like to be hands-on, so it's not easy finding something for everyone to do. Fortunately, three of them have administrative components to their jobs in addition to their on-ice coaching responsibilities, so that keeps them busy.

There is a definite pecking order on the coaching staff. For example, the birthday boy, Viktor Suchov, is my number three behind my right-hand man, Fedor Kanareykin, and the second assistant, Viktor Korolev. Suchov never played in the top league, but he's well regarded locally for his scoring exploits when Magnitogorsk was in the second league. He's really the antithesis of how Yushkevich describes the typical Russian coach. A pleasant man with a terrific smile, he's the prototypical players' coach, who enjoys working after practice with players on their offensive games. He also does our travel plans, coordinates per diems, manages the hotel registration and bus schedules while we're on the road, and supervises the strength-training circuits set up by the fitness coach.

Kanareykin played with Spartak and the Soviet Wings until the early 1990s, when the Russian Ice Hockey Federation gave him permission to play in Austria, with three-quarters of his salary paid back to the federation. This was a common practice in those days, a means for the federation to generate additional funds by "renting" players to foreign teams. Fedor speaks a reasonable amount of English, but not enough to effectively handle the translation. He's an upbeat, outgoing person, and ultra positive. I have yet to see him get angry. Maybe this is the exclusive territory of the head coach in Russia. Fedor knows the league very well, and that helps me because we'll often sit down and I'll present him with some of my tactical ideas. He'll then give me his feedback as to how he thinks they may work.

Viktor Korolev (no relation to Igor Korolev) is a former goalie in the Russian league who, paradoxically, doesn't want to work with the goalies, which is why we added a goalie coach in midsummer. Korolev prefers to coach all positions, and his energy in practice is high. He loves to jump into a drill and provide "coach resistance" to give the drill a more gamelike feel, which is a good thing, except he often pays the price by getting run over or knocked down. His commitment is admirable, but he really needs to wear a helmet! A holdover from Marek Sykora's staff, Korolev is also our statistics man and provides me with our game stats.

Our goalie coach, Yuri Shundrov, played for Sokol Kiev and joined our staff after training camp was already underway. I remember him playing for several Russian "Select" teams that toured Canada in the 1980s when I coached the national team. As a goalie,

Yuri was a gambler who relied heavily on instinct. His style was to be very aggressive, as opposed to the majority of Russian goalies, who played way back in their nets. My hope is that Yuri doesn't coach the goalies to play the way he did because he'd make Jacques Plante, who famously wandered out of the crease, look stationary by comparison. Shundrov says or does little at our on-ice practices. He has three coaching poses: a Ken Dryden lean-on-the-stick position, a pose where he places his stick across his back as he leans against the boards, and finally The Thinker, where he leans on the boards with his chin firmly planted in his hand. All three give you the impression that he can hardly wait for practice to end.

I am most suspicious of the final member of our coaching staff, Viktor Gudzik, our fitness and strength coach, who seems to pride himself on his recovery techniques. I wonder about his methods, though. He passes out pills and gives injections that no one seems to know much about – other than that they don't seem to run afoul of the league policy on drug testing. In North America, team doctors generally coordinate the entire area of fitness training, injury rehabilitation, and recovery, whereas in Russia it seems that our doctor, masseurs, and fitness coach all work independently from one another. During summer training our masseurs were worried about a couple of the weight-lifting exercises that Gudzik assigned, thinking they did more harm than good, but they didn't voice their concerns, even though they may have to deal with the resulting injuries. I'm trying to stop myself from interfering in this area because I know that this side of Russian hockey is steeped in the old Soviet tradition and probably isn't going to change, no matter what I say or do. Still, a couple of my players have warned me to be wary of Gudzik's heavy reliance on the pharmaceuticals. Frankly, he also plays politics too much for my liking. It's noteworthy that he didn't join us for our camp in Germany back in July because he couldn't get a visa – something to do with substances that he either took in or out of Germany a few years back that have him on the "no-entry" list right now.

The final member of our medical staff is team doctor Mikhail Novikov – or Super-Vrach (Super-Doc) as I call him. Over the years he's developed a wealth of orthopedic experience, but his specialty, believe it or not, is gynecology. So here we are, an all-male team, and our full-time team doctor is a gynecologist. Some things are probably just not worth thinking about.

October 12

We chartered into Siberia to Novokuznetsk, just north of Mongolia, and saw snow on the higher elevations for the first time. Winter is on its way, but I wasn't expecting it this soon, so when I was out running today in shorts, in the snow, my outfit drew more than a few long stares. Jogging isn't common in Russia to begin with, so jogging in the snow must be unprecedented.

The buzz in Russian hockey circles these days is that Lada Togliatti, one of the better teams in the league, may downsize its roster during the ten-day November break in our schedule, or when the player transfer window opens again. Even in Russia, where nothing should surprise me any more, no one really believes this could happen. The newspapers were reporting that the Lada car company would prefer to invest more money in Formula One auto racing, which makes sense on one level, since that's their primary business. They also say the team may soon fire head coach Peter Vorobiev. Two seasons ago, eight coaches were fired before Christmas. On that level, it sounds just like the NHL.

Velichkin, our GM, is with us on the trip and wanted to speak to the team before tonight's game to remind them that it was

Rashnikov's birthday and that a win would be a nice present. We took our pre-game meal in the arena restaurant, and in the middle of our private video session a few of the Novokuznetsk players wandered through our room to get to their dining room. Not much surprises me any more. Rashnikov is going to be happy because we won 6-2.

October 17

Today we flew to Moscow after a 4-1 win over Novosibirsk; everyone was excited about playing the defending champions Moscow Dynamo. It'll be the final game of the first round, and the way the Russian schedule works, you play every team once and then in the second round you play all the same teams in the reverse order. We played Dynamo in our tournament at the end of August, but this is the first time we've seen them since then. We stayed at the Hotel Ukrainia, which has security at the entrance just the way airports do. You walk in, they X-ray your luggage, and then you walk through a metal-detecting scanner. Fedor Kanareykin isn't with us. He stayed behind in Magnitogorsk because he's experiencing high-blood pressure and the doctors want to keep him in hospital for testing.

October 18

What a day. We were playing Moscow Dynamo at seven o'clock, and had some downtime at the arena before the game. I was talking, through my translator, to my assistant coaches and asked them, "What's the plan for after the game, in terms of a meal?" We had about an hour-and-a-half drive from Moscow Stadium to the airport, so I was assuming we were going to get some food for the bus. Oh yes, we were. I said, "Terrific, what are we going to get?" They said, "We're going to get McDonald's." "Well, okay, fast food, I guess that'll work. When are we going to pick it up?" The answer: "Oh, don't worry, we've already got it."

I said, "What? It's four-thirty and you've already got the food? Where is it?" Well, we have a guy who works for us in Moscow. If you're an out-of-town team, you have a Moscow liaison that books your hotel, supplies you with sticks, etc. etc. Anyway, Roman is the guy. I said, "Where does Roman have the food?" "In the trunk of his car." Imagine now, it's four-thirty in the afternoon. The game will be over at nine-thirty or ten. "Do you realize that's five to six hours? That food is going to be a little bit cold. Couldn't we just arrange to pick it up after the game and send someone in a taxi to get it? The McDonald's is only about four blocks away from the arena." But when I said that, they looked at me as if I were from another planet. "Why would we send a taxi to pick it up?" I said, "Because it would be hot, because it would be fresher." Nope, can't do it that way.

So the game ended, we got on the bus, and sure enough, on everybody's seat was this little bag of McDonald's food – stone cold. And there was no problem. Not even one complaint. I'm thinking, Somebody's going to say something. I said to my translator, Igor, "If somebody says something, let me know." But no, we'd won the game in dramatic fashion and everybody was so happy with the win that the cold food was just fine. So we bused across town eating the coldest hamburgers and french fries you've ever tasted in your life.

I just couldn't understand why they wouldn't do it differently. There was time, after the game, for Roman to go and pick it up. But they do it their way because they want to get it done and over with. That's one of the things I've noticed here. They just want to get things looked after so that they have nothing on their minds and can go out during the game and have a smoke behind the rink or do something like that.

Two of my coaches are smokers, and they sneak out all the time for a smoke. Usually they'll come into my office after the period, we talk for a minute or two about what went on, and then they disappear for a smoke. Sometimes they take longer than they should. Then I'm left thinking, When are they coming back, because I want to talk to the team about a couple of things. Eventually I go in the dressing room, shut the door, and start talking to the players – and of course, when the door's closed, they won't come in. So sometimes I've literally locked my assistant coaches outside the door because I can't wait for them any longer. But they've adjusted. They didn't quit smoking, but they now can inhale an entire cigarette in about two drags.

It was quite a night on the ice as well. We had a difficult time with the referee and had to endure a couple of five-on-threes in the regulation game. We pulled our goalie, down 2-1, and scored to tie it up 2-2 in the last minute. Then, with ten seconds to go the referee gave us another penalty, so we went into overtime, not down five-on-four, but four-on-three. But we survived the four-on-three in overtime and then Malkin scored to win it 3-2.

With two goals and one assist, Malkin was the show. Dynamo's coach is also coaching the Russian Olympic team, and if he had any doubts about choosing Malkin for his team, he must have erased them tonight. Malkin had a stretch of five games in a row where he didn't get a point. It was around the time he hurt his shoulder, but it was more than just that. Like every young player, when the puck wasn't going in for him, he tried to do more and more by himself and ended up getting less and less done. Also, I think he was distracted by the fact that the NHL season had started; Alexander Ovechkin was in Washington and here he was still in Magnitogorsk. I watched him carefully in practice and I don't think I was seeing anything that wasn't there. He wasn't as outgoing or happy as usual. In the last three games, though, he's really got it back in gear. He's back to sharing the puck and playing his game. A third of the way through the season, he really is the best player in the league.

Altogether, we've played seventeen games now and ended the first round in first place, with a record of 11-2-2-2 for thirty-nine points. Here, you get three points for a win, two for an overtime win, one for an overtime loss or a tie, and of course zero for a loss in regulation. In the NHL they have shootouts to decide regular-season games, but won't use them in the playoffs. Here, it's just the opposite. They'll have shootouts to decide playoff games, but ties are okay in the regular season. It's just another example of how things differ here.

October 19

I had one of our team drivers take Linda and me for a tour across the Ural River to see the steel mill up close, and it was like walking through a time portal. All the apartments were built around 1930 and were covered in coal dust from years of smelting steel. The steel mills are monstrous in size, and from the outside look as if they're well past their prime. Inside, I'm told, it's a different story. Apparently they're using computer-operated machinery to create a higher grade of steel, and their product is much in demand.

Magnitogorsk was originally settled centuries ago by Bashkir farmers, who raised cattle on the side of the river. The Russians came two hundred years ago, originally for military purposes. In the middle of the eighteenth century they discovered a rich iron ore deposit on the side of what they called the Magnitka Mountain and started to mine the ore, using mostly serfs as labour. Eventually, the village of Magnitaya became a one-industry town. Progress ground to a halt during the civil war between the Red and White armies, but when Joseph Stalin came to power he transplanted more than ten thousand settlers to the area and they started to build the city and the steel plant. Over time the ore deposits were exhausted, so now they import both ore and coal from other parts of Russia to fire the furnaces.

From our apartment you can see the effluents billowing up into the atmosphere, and it makes you wonder what the air quality was like before they began their environmental initiatives, which according to the people I ask have been reduced by a third over the past few years. Some nights we sleep with the windows open and awaken to the smell of coal smoke because the wind has shifted. It leaves a black film on the window ledges and we've noticed our shirts and sweater collars get a ring around them very quickly.

October 22

An old friend of mine, Bjorn Kinding, arrived in Magnitogorsk today after a nightmarish day of travel that left him stuck in the Moscow airport for twenty-four hours. We had snow Thursday and Friday and the airport was closed all day Friday and most of Saturday. This amount of snow wouldn't close any airport in the rest of the world, but it does here. Our translator, Igor, said that the same thing happens every winter: the first snowfall catches everyone off guard. Bjorn brought a care package for Linda so that she could begin some Christmas baking. He's Swedish but has lived in Canada for most of the past ten years; his wife coaches figure skaters at the Royal Glenora club in Edmonton. Bjorn has done work for Hockey Canada and for the Japanese federation, and now he's preparing a report on Russian youth hockey development for coaches in Sweden. He's going to spend eight days with us, camped out in our tiny apartment.

October 23

Gennady Velichkin spoke to me about bringing up a few of our farm-team players, one of whom is his son, Igor. At this time our team is healthy, we're winning, and even our extra players are competing hard to get into a game, so I tell him no, we're not changing anything right now. I'm sensing that this is going to be a problem all year long. Sure, he wants us to win, but he also wants us to win with his son in our lineup. The problem is that Igor Velichkin isn't ready to play in our starting group, unless we really run into injuries. Velichkin's lobbying really bothers my assistant, Fedor Kanareykin, because Fedor's son, Leonid, plays in the Moscow Dynamo system and had to earn his place through hard work. Over and over, Fedor tells me that he never pulled strings to advance his son's career. That he's so bothered by Velichkin's pressuring is probably a good thing for me. I'll have an ally in Fedor if the pressure ramps up over the course of the season.

October 24

The second round of Super League play began today, and its reverse order means we start at home against Moscow Dynamo, the team we just beat in Moscow. Fedor Kanareykin was released from hospital yesterday after an eight-day stay because of concerns over an irregular heartbeat. The timing couldn't be better for him either, because his son Leonid plays defence for Dynamo and Fedor had already missed the first game of our home-and-home series with the defending champs. We won again 4-2; our rink was sold out and the fans just loved it. It wasn't that long ago that the only thing they knew about these famous Moscow teams was what they read in the newspaper or saw on TV. Now they see them live and in person, and getting the better of them means a lot.

There's been a lot of talk about the Olympics; Vladimir Krikunov, who coaches Moscow Dynamo, was asked at the press conference after the game if any of the Magnitogorsk players were possible candidates. He played it very coy. He said, "We've got a list formed and nothing has really changed." The list is still a secret, but we believe that Malkin, Kaigorodov, Atyushov, and maybe Chistov are on the long Olympic list.

Now that we're into the second third of the season, I've been here long enough that I can speak some Russian on the bench. It really helps a lot. In the dressing room I mix Russian and English. I know the Russian words for "breakout" and "passive forechecking," so I can very often get my point across with broken Russian and English. I can't go into a long dissertation with a player. For that, I need Igor or Dmitri or one of my English-speaking guys to help me.

If I had to, I've probably got ten players who are capable of being coached completely in English, including both my goalies, plus four guys on defence: Boulin, Yushkevich, Varlamov, and Boikov. Up front, it gets a little sparse. Igor Korolev is fluent. Kaigorodov speaks a little, but not enough. Gusmanov, Chistov, and Alexander Savchenkov are all okay. Kaigorodov is really working at his English and becoming more proficient. He's not there yet, but he's come a long way. As for Malkin, I can see no signs of his English improving at all. He seems to understand some of what I'm saying, but most of the time he's looking over to the translator. So Malkin hasn't gotten over that bridge. I'm not going to worry about that yet, but I'll make sure he works on it after Christmas. He's just a young guy, and right now he's having fun playing hockey. He comes to practice with a big smile on his face and goes out and just has fun. In the NHL the young rookies all get designer suits; soon their tastes get expensive and refined and they're pretty polished. Well, Malkin is a guy who wears the blue jeans and the tennis shoes and a variety of different baseball hats. He's unpolished. He's like a kid off the farm – and that's what he's going to be like when he hits the NHL. You'll see a kid who's a little rough around the edges, but you'll like him because he'll be an easy guy to talk to, a really good kid.

October 28

Today a CTV network crew from Moscow arrived for a short visit. When Linda heard they were coming she asked Ellen Pinchuk, their reporter, to bring us some fresh vegetables, so when Ellen arrived she brought four heads of lettuce. We're starting to get concerned because it looks as if there'll be a very narrow selection of produce in the grocery stores as the weather gets colder and winter closes in. There are just a couple of different types of cabbage and tomatoes, cucumbers, and big pulpy carrots that aren't very tasty, so making a salad is getting to be more difficult.

We played at home against Novokuznetsk and won 2-1 in a rather mediocre performance. Afterwards the CTV crew trailed us to our favourite haunt, the pizza place I discovered soon after I arrived. That, for me, was a major find. We were driving downtown to go to a press conference and I saw this Baskin-Robbins ice cream parlour, but there was also a brand-new sign that read "Pizza House." I said to Igor: "Turn the car around right now so we can see what this is all about." We went inside and learned that the person who owned the Baskin-Robbins decided that in the wintertime he needed a second business, because ice cream sales fell off once it got too cold, so he turned half his place into a pizza parlour. I was just dumbfounded when we tried the pizza because it was absolutely terrific. I was impressed with everything about it. They used a high grade of cheese and made thin-crust pizza that was comparable to a lot of the pizza parlours I've visited around the world. So far, I haven't seen much in Magnitogorsk that really knocked my socks off, but this pizza place did. We go there at least once a week, and if Linda's away I'll go there twice a week – and boy, it's great.

At first I had to explain what I wanted, which was difficult because none of the people who work there spoke any English. So for the first few visits, I used hand signals and got my dictionary out and figured out how to say "ham" and "cheese" and words like that. Now when I go in, it's automatic. I walk up, I smile. They ask if I want *malinky*, which is small, or *bolshoi*, which is big. I always want *bolshoi*. They know Coach King is here, and since they've figured out who I am and what I do I get asked to sign autographs and such.

Over the years I've come to learn the difference between good and bad pizza – which I blame on the bizarre, burning-the-candle-at-both-ends hockey lifestyle. You can go to a small town in almost any province in Canada or anywhere in Europe, and late at night after a game there aren't a lot of places where you can go for dinner. A lot of the fast-food joints are closed, but pizza places tend to stay open later. So early in my coaching career, when I'd be looking for a place to eat with my coaching staff, I discovered that no matter where you go, everybody's got a late-night pizza place in town.

October 31

Bjorn Kinding left to go home today. When he and I got on the elevator from our eighth-floor apartment, the door closed but the elevator didn't move. We were trapped there with all his luggage. And since I was planning to go for my jog after he left, I didn't even have my cellphone with me. Thankfully, after about ten minutes Linda noticed that we weren't downstairs getting into the taxi and realized that the banging noise she heard must be coming from the two of us, trapped in the elevator. So she phoned our translator, who came over and talked to the superintendent, and they eventually got the elevator doors open and fixed the thing. Bjorn and I couldn't wait for that because he had a flight to catch, so we carried the luggage down eight flights of stairs, laughing all the way.

November 2

We flew Pterodactyl Air to Samara and then took a one-hour bus ride to Togliatti, whose team is the talk of the league right now. Lada, the car company that sponsors the team, is involved in Formula One racing, but they want to up the ante and get in at a much higher level. They believe there's a higher payoff for them in motor racing, given that they're a car company, but it means the hockey team will have to continue with a far more limited budget. There's also talk that Lada plans to drop their women's soccer team, which is one of the best in Russia, and that volleyball may be in trouble too. This will be a blow to the city of Togliatti and its various sports, not to mention a possible mid-season changing of the guard in our league because they're planning to dump about two-thirds of their players, even though we're not even halfway through the schedule.

When I first heard about the possibility, I couldn't believe what I was hearing. In fact, I said to our guys, "You can't tell me this is really going to happen this year. Maybe it's an idle threat." "No," they answered, "it's really going to happen." Imagine if the Toronto Maple Leafs, halfway through the season and in a contending position, tried to dump all their contracts. Imagine a team cleaning house, but not at the trading deadline. It's only two months into the season, they're in the top half of the league, and nicely on target to make the playoffs. It left me at a loss for words, and the outcome of the game didn't surprise me either. We played to a 0-0 tie with Lada, and their players all played hard. Clearly, they're busy trying to market themselves to other Super League teams, if Lada follows up on its promises.

November 4

Continuing on Pterodactyl Air to Ufa for our last game before the November break, we were worried as a coaching staff that our players were thinking more about their upcoming ten-day break than this, our last game. Our fears were validated when we played poorly and lost 4-2. I was disappointed in the result, but my message to the players after the game was mostly positive: I told them that they'd worked hard since June 28 and deserved this break; that they should enjoy some time with their families and then come back ready to go.

November 7

Naturally, the players aren't the only ones who are going to enjoy the break. Two days ago Linda and I flew Magnitogorsk-Moscow-Frankfurt, rented a car, and drove to Augsburg to spend a whirlwind two-and-a-half days with our son Scott and his wife, Katherine. Of course, the business of hockey is never very far away, especially not in the age of cellphones. Today my translator, Igor, called to say that the rumours were true – Lada *was* dumping contracts – and that we had a chance to pick up Ilya Vorobiev, the son of Peter Vorobiev, the team's coach. Ilya isn't a flashy player, but he's a gritty competitor and plays all three forward positions, so we decided to go ahead.

In Augsburg I saw Scott play, and as usual he impressed me with his intelligence and playmaking abilities. Scott is playing for his third team in three years. The offers for his services just keep getting better and better; he's a top-ten scorer in the German league and it looks as if he'll be playing in the DEL for years to come. Even though Augsburg is struggling and may miss the playoffs, Scott played a strong game.

November 8

On the way home now again after an all-too-short vacation, we flew Frankfurt-Moscow-Magnitogorsk and once again arrived at five a.m. I'm not sure I've ever arrived here other than at five a.m., and can't say that I'm getting used to it either. Travel in the NHL is challenging. When I was with the national team we had some marathon days, but I've never had a year in which I spent quite so much time in airports and on airplanes. There was a familiar face to meet us when we touched down in Moscow, however: Dean McIntosh from Hockey Canada was waiting to accompany us to Magnitogorsk. He'll spend the next eight days sharing our apartment while he studies Russian youth hockey development in the same manner as Bjorn Kinding. Our place is small, but we're happy for the company and not just because Dean also brought the obligatory care package: English books, DVDs, magazines, and some food favourites, including chocolate chips so that Linda can bake her special oatmeal chocolate chip cookies.

November 10

Play doesn't resume in the league for another six days, while the Karjala Cup competition is finishing in Finland. We have three players competing there, but for the rest it's back to two-a-day practices with one hour of dryland training sessions mixed in. I'm disappointed that The Fish, our talented but mercurial forward, won't be involved. He's had just a so-so season thus far, not at all the top-six forward I thought we had here. He showed up for work today with a broken toe. My assistants tell me that it occurred during an off-ice drinking incident. Apparently this isn't the first time this has happened to The Fish – and alcohol is usually involved.

I try to follow the NHL news more or less regularly, and one of the major problems this season is an epidemic of groin and/or abdominal injuries. I'm no doctor, but we don't have nearly as many groin strains here and I'm wondering if that has something to do with the tremendous strength the Russian players develop in their quadriceps. This is an across-the-board thing, too; it isn't limited to just a handful of players. To a man, the leg strength of a Russian player will amaze you. The quadriceps muscles, which deliver so much power to the stride, are huge on virtually every one of them. Right from the time they turn eight or nine years old, they do an immense amount of work to build up their leg strength. The youngsters don't use weights because their bones are in an important growth phase. Instead they do lots of deep squat work such as the duck-walk. They also play tag or pass around a basketball or medicine ball while in the squat position. The results are evident when you see them skate. They train for strength, but they really emphasize quick, explosive power that affects both the start and the acceleration in skating. Our team spends a little bit of every day working on leg strength, even on game days. And now, in the middle of this break, the routine is greatly enhanced. Every day until we start up again our players will complete two hundred hurdle jumps, lift several tons of weights, and run a few kilometres over a four-day, high-intensity training block, just to top up their fitness levels.

November 12

I've had to change my running routine because it's become just too difficult to run in the mornings. It's too dark now, and the roads are a mine field. They're so uneven that you really have to step carefully in case you end up in a giant pothole and turn your ankle. So I've tried a couple of afternoon runs this past week and it works much, much better. And because it's later in the day I get to see more of everything; one of the more dramatic changes in the landscape is that construction on our new arena is moving along pretty well. They have all the pilings in now, which is the first and most important step before winter really socks in.

November 13

Ever since he arrived a few days ago, Dean McIntosh has been haunting the arena from morning until night, watching practices, interviewing people, and compiling as much data as possible in his short visit. This is what being a hockey coach is all about: you run your own practice and then you sit in the stands and watch someone else do theirs. One of my primary reasons for coming to Magnitogorsk was to observe the Russian training methods from an insider's point of view. It's what Bjorn Kinding wanted to do; it's what Dean is doing now. And during this break in the schedule I too have had a lot more time to see what I've come to view as our hockey factory in action. Both Dean and Bjorn learned what I'd already discovered in my first four months here – that the system for training young players is unique and far different from what we're accustomed to in North America.

On our team we have a handful of players, including Malkin and Kaigorodov, who were developed through the Metallurg

Magnitogorsk youth hockey school. And when they call it a school, they mean it literally. They approach hockey the same way we in North America approach education for our children. They're on the ice every day for practices supervised by trained, full-time professional coaches. If you're good enough to attend the hockey school, you spend half your day in the classroom and half your day on the ice.

The youth hockey programs are divided into two distinct age groups – ten and under and eleven and over. The younger players play two tournaments per season, but they don't play in leagues. They're on the ice for an eight-month period, from September 1 until the end of April, five times a week, with the sixth day spent in a dryland training session. Once they reach the age of eleven, things change. They start to travel all over the region to play games. Russia is divided into six regions for hockey; ours is called Ural-West Siberia region. Some of these road trips are long and rigorous. For example, to play Omsk, which is in our region, our preteen players travel four hours by bus to Chelyabinsk and then take a twelve- to thirteen-hour train ride just to play two games – and then they travel home again. These are eleven-year-olds, remember.

The older age group (eleven to sixteen) starts their season two months earlier – on July 1, with a month of dryland training. On-ice sessions start on August 1 and continue until the middle of May. The practices are ninety minutes long and the boys are on the ice six times a week. In a ten-and-a-half-month season, they get in about one hundred practices, one hundred off-ice dryland training sessions, and thirty-six league games. They'll also play twelve to fifteen exhibition games and up to a dozen playoff games. Last year Magnitogorsk won the Russian championship for boys born in 1991 and 1992, so these players probably put in a total of 240 hours on the ice, invested another 150 hours in dryland training, played about 50 to 55 games, and logged a ton of travel miles because our region is so spread out. It's a staggering commitment and explains a lot – their stoicism in the face of a heavy practice schedule and their ability to shrug off the long, tedious travel days that are a fact of life when playing professionally in such a huge country.

In most Russian hockey organizations it's common for the same coach to stay with the same boys for a decade – from the time they start, at age five or six, to the time they turn sixteen. This sort of year-to-year continuity allows the coach to have a real impact on the players' development over a ten-year span. Most of the coaches in the Magnitogorsk system have some higher education combined with some advanced playing experience, which makes them very competent.

Cost, which is such a factor in Canada and the United States, is negligible here. Ice hockey fees are about $5 a month, and at the age of thirteen and above the organization will provide all equipment. There's no women's hockey in most cities, and I'm told the future doesn't look good. Even for the boys, youth hockey tends to be a rather elite sport; they winnow out the average and below-average talents early on. The goal for every boy (and his coach) is to make it to the Super League, but if they show only limited potential, there aren't a lot of alternatives – no recreational or house leagues as we have in Canada. Their only real option is to play outdoors, unsupervised – and most cities have outdoor rinks so that youngsters who get dropped from the elite stream can play shinny. But there are no coaches, referees, or league structure. It's simply for fun – and if the boys want to play, they need to keep the ice clear of snow themselves.

For the high-end kids, one of the biggest differences in training methods is the amount of time spent on a single drill. Often they'll run the same drill for twenty minutes. They divide the ice into three zones, with the kids rotating from zone to zone; in a one-hour session they'll spend twenty minutes in each zone. The coaches believe that "repetition is the mother of learning." To see how focused and disciplined these young players are as they repeat and repeat the same skill set in a drill is something to behold. The coaches tend to be patient for the first few minutes as the youngsters adjust or adapt to the drill, but once they understand it, the coaches demand tempo. They spend hours and hours on skating and puck-control skills; it's common for a young player to have a puck on his stick for at least half the practice. They also balance full-ice and small-area drills so that the youngsters work on all aspects of skating and puck control. Most teams are made up of five units of five, with the top two units doing a lot of the competitions against each other. As well, the top two units appear to get a little more of the coaches' attention since they're the most likely to move up to the next level. And a coach's evaluation is based mainly on how many players he'll graduate to the elite levels beyond the age of sixteen. It's simple: develop several good players and you're a good coach, with all the rewards and privileges attached to that. The coaches who are recognized and rewarded in Magnitogorsk are the ones who developed the Malkins and the Kaigorodovs, the young stars of the Super League.

Once a player reaches the age of seventeen he's eligible to play in the Super League, but few are ready at this age. By rule, every team must dress two nineteen-year-olds in their lineup. As well, nearly every Super League team has a farm team made up of seventeen-, eighteen-, and nineteen-year-old players, who compete in the third league, a men's league, where the calibre of play is good enough to stretch them to improve.

But what I like best about their approach is the time they spend on offensive skills and tactics. For example, when they do simple one-on-one drills with youngsters, the coaches focus much more on offensive than defensive skills. They continually push the kids to find new solutions in one-on-one play. They work on skating and puck control so much that these young players develop confidence in challenging the defender and stretch themselves to be innovative in small areas. They'll initiate a move on a defender, and then right in the middle of the move they'll have the ability to react to the defender's response and find a solution. Often, early in practice, I'll have my players pair up and compete in small areas one-on-one. Then I'll just stand back and enjoy the fun. They have such quick hands and can move the puck as if it were glued on their stick blade. Along with excellent skating agility, it really makes defending a challenge. They're rarely stationary, they feel checking pressure, they give so many deceptive fakes, and they can change direction on a dime. Combine this with great puck protection skills and it explains how they appear to practically evaporate on the defender. There's an old hockey proverb: When checking, you need to either get the chicken (the man) or the egg (the puck), but don't come up with just feathers. When checking a Russian player, you'll often come up with just feathers.

November 15

Tomorrow the schedule resumes after the ten-day international break, which allowed the national teams from all across Europe to get together and train. In an Olympic year, the importance of doing so is clearly enhanced. We're three games into the second round of the schedule and are sitting in first place. After all that early-season angst, everyone is pleased by our progress, but the player movement during this first transfer window may shift the balance of power in the league and should make the rest of the second round more challenging.

As advertised, Lada – which was standing seventh out of eighteen teams – did sell eleven players into the marketplace, thereby reducing their payroll by between US$7 and $9 million. In no professional league I've ever been associated with do you get a team that's in seventh place and doing very well suddenly release eleven players to the league.

Lada kept only seven players from their original team and promoted a number of players from their farm team. They also borrowed a handful of players from other teams in the league – young players from your farm club or from the end of your roster who can't play regularly for you. Because we want to develop those players, we loaned two to Lada – a young defenceman, Rinat Ibragimov, plus a young forward, Igor Velichkin, the son of our general manager, Gennady Velichkin.

There are a lot of father-son combinations in the NHL as well, but this exchange was a first for me. Lada sent us Pavel Vorobiev, the son of their coach, and we sent them Igor Velichkin, the son of our general manager. It wasn't as if Gennady Velichkin traded his son because we still own his rights and we'll get him back for the start of next season. Gennady had talked to me twice about bringing him up, and twice I overruled him. I said, "I just can't do that because we've got extra players on our team, fighting to get into the lineup, and I owe them my loyalty – that if a spot opens up, they'll get the first crack at it."

Presumably, that brought Velichkin to the point where he thought, My son's not going to play for our team, so I have to get him in somewhere else if he wants to play in the Super League this year. But it was hard for him to make that move. They're a close family. They have a daughter and a son and Igor has been under his father's wing for a long time. It's obviously hard for Gennady to see Igor fly off on his own. Fedor Kanareykin, my assistant, figures that by next year, sending Igor off to play elsewhere won't be an option; it'll be mandatory that he play for us. That will be problematic because we both know that he's an average player with an ambitious father. That sort of volatile mix never works out well for the head coach.

The good news is that Lada is famous in Russia as one of the hardest places to play, not because it isn't a great city or a great organization or a great place to play, but because the coach there, Peter

Vorobiev, is known for being the hardest of the Russian coaches. He pushes the players to the extreme. So Igor is leaving the nest and he's going to a team where you need to put your boots on and get the lunch pail out because you're going to work. The Sutter brothers would look like easygoing Jacques Demers compared with Peter Vorobiev. He is one tough customer and one accomplished coach. There was talk earlier in the year that Lada might fire him, but he just turned their team around and they won eight in a row. Now that they've downsized, it'll be interesting to see how well they do.

Khimik, meanwhile, was floundering after losing Kovalchuk to the NHL, so their response was to absorb six players from Lada and add two others, which increased their depth and made them an instant contender. They have a serious team now. The chemistry has to unfold, but now they have four very strong lines, whereas before you could take advantage of their third and fourth lines.

Everybody's following Kovalchuk's success in the NHL and there are about seventeen teams smiling, because he's scoring his goals for Atlanta and not for Khimik. When they lost Kovalchuk it looked as if their team had lost hope. That's why they went and got eight or nine players from Lada, including Alexander Semin, a very good player who is a top prospect in the Washington Capitals organization returning to Russia because of a contract dispute.

Severstal also added five new players, one of whom came from our team, Sergei Arekaev, a player I couldn't get into our lineup on a regular basis. Avangard Omsk added Milan Novak, an excellent scorer from the Czech league, and paid a big transfer fee to get him. We talked about Jason Krog, the former Duck, and Rem Murray, the former Oiler, but there was no one in whom we thought we should invest an import card – at least, not right now.

November 16

Dean left this morning, and later in the day we played and beat Molot Perm 4-0. Molot's players haven't been paid since August, yet they continue to play hard. Some of their players borrowed tape from our players, and the trainers told us that the players were even buying their own soap and shampoo for showers. Remember, a few months ago, the newspapers reported that the president of the Molot hockey and basketball teams left unexpectedly for Cyprus with US$450,000. She's back in Perm now, but nobody seems to know what happened to the money. Or they don't tell me when I ask. Everyone simply shrugs their shoulders and says "This is Russia" – as if that should explain everything; as if I've been here long enough to understand that there are some questions better left unasked and some answers better left unsaid.

November 17

Vladislav Boulin, one of my real warriors on defence, dropped by for a visit today as a pre-emptive strike. He wanted to tip me off to the fact that Gudzik would be coming by to complain about his not taking the pills Gudzik prescribed for him. Usually Gudzik rewards that act of insubordination by accusing the player of drinking or being overweight. I've already caught on to Gudzik's act, so I told Boulin not to worry, I'd handle it. Sure enough, later in the day Gudzik came by, demanding that Boulin be fined or benched for being overweight. Thankfully, we weigh our players every ten days or so and I happened to have the latest results in my briefcase, which I produced to show that Boulin's weight hadn't fluctuated at all. That ended the conversation abruptly and Gudzik left, grumbling something in Russian that I didn't understand – but that probably wasn't complimentary.

I tell the players that, when presented with one of Gudzik's cocktails, they should press him on what they're putting into their bodies. Sadly, they're brought up not to question authority. Last year we had five players attend a national junior camp and two failed the drug test. No wonder the players are worried about the supplements they're being asked to ingest.

November 18

Tonight we got our second chance to play CSKA, the famous Central Red Army team, and we were looking for a little revenge. We lost to them 4-3 back in early October (only the second of our three losses to date). Our rink was sold out and anticipation was high, as Red Army is on a roll. In their last six games they've scored thirty goals and allowed only twelve. We're in first place and they're in third, but they're only five points behind us in the standings, so with a victory in regulation (worth three points), they could make up a lot of ground. It set up a great game, and for us it was a great game. We won 6-2 in an emotional and fast-paced match.

Viktor Tikhonov isn't behind the Red Army bench any more. He's the team president now; the coach is Slava Bykov, who was a national team stalwart for a dozen years but finished his playing career in Switzerland, even though he had a chance to play in the NHL for the Quebec Nordiques. Tikhonov didn't come down from Moscow for the game, so I didn't get to see my old adversary from the Cold War days. I'm interested in knowing what his life is like now that he no longer coaches. He was always a career coach, and career coaches generally make reluctant administrators. Also, he's part of the old world, and the Russian sports system is now run by an ex-player – Slava Fetisov – who was at odds with Tikhonov for most of his playing career.

Even without Tikhonov behind the bench, it was a thrill to coach against Red Army because, for years, they formed the nucleus of the Olympic team, along with a sprinkling of players from Moscow Dynamo. So Red Army really represents a lot of the history of Russian hockey. To get back at them, after the way they handled us in their building earlier in the season, was sweet indeed.

November 19

The big news in the papers here is that Moscow Dynamo has filed suit against the Washington Capitals in U.S. court in an attempt to bring back Alexander Ovechkin. Dynamo is seeking to have a U.S. court enforce a Russian arbitration board ruling that Dynamo, not the Capitals, rightfully own Ovechkin's contractual rights for this season. Ovechkin left Dynamo back in April after helping them win the Super League title to sign with Omsk, but his Omsk contract contained an out clause that let him back out of the deal by mid-July if he decided to join the Caps – which he did. Here's where it got complicated: the Russians ruled that Dynamo was allowed to match the Omsk contract offer – of US$1.8 million – and the Dynamo contract apparently didn't have an out clause. And Ovechkin has been every bit as good as Sidney Crosby in the NHL, so Washington isn't the least bit interested in letting him go.

Dynamo, meanwhile, is really struggling. They've lost six of eight games, which may explain the timing of the initiative.

Of course, we think it's all a figment of somebody's imagination. That's what our guy Velichkin said anyway: that there's no way Ovechkin's coming back under any circumstances. Dynamo is just under a lot of pressure to get something done, which is why they're chasing this dream of trying to get Ovechkin back.

Still, it's interesting for me to see things from the Russian perspective. In the NHL we'd draft Russian players and just assume that the best ones would ultimately come to North America if the opportunity presented itself. After all, the NHL was the top league in the world; it paid the highest salaries; and the amenities and lifestyle were terrific, so why wouldn't they want to come?

Now, of course, things look a little different from the other side of the fence. These Russian teams invest a lot of time and effort in player development. When they do produce a top-notch young player, who can break a game open and fill the building and make the sponsors proud to be associated with their team, it's important to keep him around as long as possible. The trouble is, they rarely hold on to their young stars for very long. They have some good-quality returning players like Alexei Morozov, who's playing for Ak Bars Kazan – and Pittsburgh could really use Morozov now. There's also Alexander Semin here, who's not bad, but he's not a big star like Malkin or Ovechkin. They need these players to stay in the league . . . for a little while anyway. There has to be some payoff for the teams that develop players over here.

A few years back, the league decreed that every team had to have a brand-new arena in place by 2007 with at least seven thousand seats – a modern arena, with TV screens and all the amenities. That was also mandated by the federation. So all the old arenas are being phased out with the teams given three to four years to get these buildings up. Neftekhimik just opened their building last night. Kazan's will be ready in mid-December. And they need more than just the aging stars to fill these new buildings; they need the young stars as well.

Velichkin also mentioned that he thought Molot's players might go on strike today. They haven't been paid since last August, and apparently they'd finally had enough and told the ownership that they're not going to play until they get their money. MVD, the police team, hasn't been paid in two months either, and they're saying there could be a showdown there as well. Apparently the sponsor for MVD had some investments go wrong and that's why he's no longer in a position to pay the players. Gad, it's complicated over here. What next?

November 21

The newspapers are full of speculation that Malkin will play for Russia at the world junior championships in Vancouver and then play in the Olympics as well. We don't want him to do both; we're afraid it will drain his emotional tank. The world junior is an intense tournament, and in any case our league doesn't break for it. The elite teams continue to play because they give up only their '86-born and '87-born players to the national junior team – a small sacrifice, given that they're not their core players. We're a little different. Malkin is our top scorer and our top player. And it's not just that he's the best '86, he's the best player period in the Russian Super League.

Selfishly, we believe he can't play in Canada from December 21 to January 6 and then go back to Turin three-and-a-half weeks later. It's too much. Imagine this: when we go into our break next month, Malkin will play in the Rosno Cup starting December 15. He would then play world junior. He would come back and play a concentrated three-and-a-half-week schedule (we'll have to make up the games we miss by going to play in the Spengler Cup over Christmas) and then play in the Olympics. Once they end, he'll have to hustle back for the last five games of our schedule before we jump into the playoffs.

So all we've asked from the federation is to make their choice and let us know. It looks as if they want him on the Olympic team, along with five or six other players from the Russian league. Malkin played for Russia in last year's world championships. He was good for them – and he's a better player now. So we hope they choose him just for the Olympics. That would be better for everybody.

November 21

We beat Spartak 5-3, but we were a little too casual in the latter stages of the game and almost let it slip through our fingers. Afterwards I talked to Spartak's two Canadians, Tyler Moss and David Ling, who sound as if they're enjoying Moscow. They told me an unbelievable story about a teammate of theirs, Rick Mrozik, and what he went through this season. Mrozik is an American, from Duluth, Minnesota, and once upon a time was a pretty good NHL prospect. But he ended up playing only two NHL games in the next ten years, so last summer, after it became clear that he was probably destined to spend the rest of his career in the minors, he and Tyler – who'd played with him on the Edmonton Oilers' minor-league affiliate – decided to try it in Russia and signed with Spartak.

In early August, in a pre-season tournament game in Perm, Mrozik was skating backwards in his own zone and fell over top of one of the Perm players. He hit his head on the ice and suffered a skull fracture – only it wasn't diagnosed as a skull fracture right away. They just told him he had a mild concussion and not to worry. But then his headaches became worse, and finally they had to admit him to hospital in Perm, where they finally diagnosed it correctly. He had to undergo brain surgery immediately to relieve the pressure from fluid on his brain. I can only imagine what he must have been feeling. A year ago, during the lockout, Sergei Zholtok died after having a heart seizure in Riga, Latvia. Every team has a doctor, but they don't have anywhere near the emergency equipment in these old arenas that they do in the NHL.

Naturally, the team returned to Moscow after the tournament ended, but Mrozik couldn't travel with them – and he couldn't travel by air at all because of the air pressure in the cabin. So after seventeen days in hospital he had to take a train back to Moscow. By then his visa had expired, and when he arrived they were checking papers on his train. He didn't have the right ones, so they took him to jail and interrogated him for the better part of two days before finally letting him go.

It took months until he was well enough to travel, and only just the other day did he get medical clearance to fly home to the United States. Before he left, he suggested he wasn't coming back. After what he went through, who could blame him?

November 23

It looks as if Yaroslav Lokomotiv will be one of our biggest challengers, and yesterday we took a 250-kilometre bus ride there from Moscow. That might take about two hours anywhere else, but here it was a four hours-plus trip because of the narrow roads and the heavy traffic, which made the going slow. Thankfully we had two buses, so the players could spread out and have lots of room.

After the pre-game meal I went down to the old city to run around the Kremlin. Normally we associate the term "Kremlin" with the seat of government in Moscow, but every major city in Russia has its own Kremlin, which refers to the fortress inside the walls of the old city. Hundreds of years ago when Moscow or Yaroslav were just small cities, people lived outside the wall, but if they were ever under attack from an enemy they sought refuge inside the Kremlin.

Yaroslav's Kremlin is unbelievable – it's old and decaying, but they've fixed it up nicely. The city is 995 years old and will celebrate its millennium in five years. When you're from Canada, you realize we're just babies as a country. Sometimes I have to pinch myself and say, Don't let this become ho-hum. The contrast was so striking – in the evening, you're at a hockey game played in a brand-new arena, built in 2002, and it's gorgeous, state-of-the-art. In the afternoon you were downtown, running around a Kremlin built in the twelfth century, with some of the original stone still there.

We won the game 2-0, and afterwards I earned a victory of a different sort. Something I said must have sunk in, because on the forty-minute bus ride out to the airport, there was a bag of McDonald's food on everybody's seat. I thought, Uh-oh, not again. But this time it was warm. Okay, it wasn't hot, but it was warm. Victory!

November 24

More proof that the players here have a different mindset from any other team I've ever been associated with. The charter from Yaroslav arrived home at three-thirty in the morning, Magnitogorsk time. We had just won two important games on the road. It was minus six outside and we told the guys that it was a good news/bad news day. The good news was we weren't going on the ice first thing in the morning. The bad news was we were going on a six-kilometre run outside, followed by an afternoon in the gym to do weights. No one blinked when they heard. No one complained. No one said anything. In some ways, I sensed they were grateful that at least they didn't have to skate. It's my fifth month here and I still find myself approaching these decisions from the point of view of a North American coach. I think: Boy, are these guys going to be peeved when they hear this. Then you walk in and they're getting changed into their running gear and it's, Ho-hum, we're going outside for a run today in the cold.

In the meantime I was reviewing the Yaroslav video, and what jumped out at me was how Malkin had very clearly played an NHL type of game that night. He was physical and solid defensively, plus he was exciting offensively. He seemed to have an endless supply of energy. I think he's learning from watching Igor Korolev and Dmitri Yushkevich, who set an excellent example for our young players every night. They compete on every shift. And they regulate the dressing room when the dressing room needs regulating. That makes it so much easier for me – or for any coach – when the standard for performance is established internally, by the players themselves. Really, the only downside to the whole day was that Travis Scott strained a groin muscle against Yaroslav and our doctor confirmed that he'll need time off for therapy. It means Konstantin Simchuk will get a chance to play again.

Nominally, we started the season with Simchuk as our number one goalie just because they knew him better here, whereas Travis Scott was a real unknown. In their minds, until Scott proved himself, Simchuk was the go-to guy. In the first couple of games I alternated back and forth, but after about two starts each Simchuk had let in five power-play goals. We've allowed only seven since then. I thought some of those goals were weak on his part. So I made the switch and thought, If Travis could get hot, I'm going with him – and that's exactly what happened. He put together a string of wins. We've won five in a row and thirteen of our last fourteen games, along with that scoreless tie against Lada. We haven't lost since early October to Red Army. Travis basically won the job. One of the keys to his game is that he's so good with the puck compared with Simchuk. Simchuk is a gambler. Travis is a more high-percentage guy in the net and handles the puck so much better. That's been the difference and it's really helped our whole game – his ability to play the puck and help out the defencemen. So he's now number one.

I've found him to be a very self-sufficient guy and really, the perfect choice for us. There's always a risk when you bring a North American player to Russia, because how he does often has little to do with his hockey-playing abilities (all the guys can play), but rather with how he adapts to his surroundings. Some players are high maintenance, but not Travis. He's been a very low-maintenance guy. He's quiet, and he likes his privacy. He reads, he listens to music, he's got his computer, and he's happy just with that. Most of the Canadian players who come over just try to get through the season and don't want to come back. I think Travis is planning to stay for a couple of years if he can. The money is really good, but also he's the right type of guy to survive in this environment. Some guys couldn't.

Magnitogorsk is the perfect place for a coach because there aren't a lot of girls and bars and things to distract your players. You don't sit around and worry about what they're doing at night because there isn't that much for them to do. It's also a very small city, so if any of the guys are out in the bar, the next day I'll know right away. My assistant manager, Oleg Kuprianov, will tell me that So-and-so was in the pub the other night because somebody would have called him to let him know. So they're under the microscope here, which works well for us. Moscow is a different story. David Ling and Tyler Moss, who play for Spartak, told me that a lot of their players have a good social life outside of hockey, and that sometimes it hurts their team. We don't have that problem here.

November 25

From our apartment I can walk to the arena, which usually takes only about two minutes. The only problem is that I have to cross a busy intersection to get there, and even though it's theoretically controlled by lights, cars deliberately run the red just about every day. I've seen at least four or five accidents by now. I'm sure someone will get badly injured this winter because the drivers all drive too fast for road conditions. Linda thinks that if something happens to us over here, it will be in a car – and she's probably right. The taxis are all so old; it makes you wonder how often they replace the brake shoes. As well, you can never find a working seat belt, so when you sit in the back seat you put your hands up, ready to brace yourself against the seat just in case. Also, Linda won't ride in the elevator in our apartment building unless I'm with her. It's small and dingy and breaks down too often. She's not sure her cellphone would work in there, and since she doesn't speak Russian, who would she call to rescue her anyway? Even when I'm with her, we'll often walk up the 133 steps (not counting the landings) to our apartment on the eighth floor. If nothing else, we're staying fit.

November 28

I'm home alone without Linda, who's gone to spend a week in Mexico with Andy's family. After practice Velichkin told me that MVD fired their coach today, so that's four teams now (including Salavat Yulaev, Vityaz, and Novokuznetsk) with new coaches. Tonight we won another important game, 3-2, over Ak Bars Kazan. Afterwards, Freddie Brathwaite and Ray Giroux, their two Canadian imports, asked where they could get a good pizza, so I sent them to the Pizza House. Freddie said that if he got food poisoning and couldn't play the next game it would be on my conscience. I laughed. He's a great goalie and an even better person.

November 30

We flew to St. Petersburg today for the first time all season and discovered that all three major ice facilities were booked for the World Team Handball Championships, so we'll play our game in the small fifteen-hundred-seat Red Army arena, which has a North American-sized ice surface.

During our pre-game skate I could tell that our players were concerned about the small ice surface and the fact that the quality of the ice is poor, which could be an equalizer in a game against a weaker opponent. After the pre-game meal, Igor, my Russian translator, and I caught the subway downtown to see the sights, including the Hermitage museum and its spectacular art collection.

Later, we won the game 7-3 – that's our highest offensive outburst of the season to date – and adjusted pretty well to the smaller-size ice. The irony didn't escape me either. My pre-game meeting was all about how to adjust our game to smaller ice, whereas when I'd come here with the Canadian national team the talk was always about adjusting to the bigger European ice surface.

December 3

Severstal Cherepovets added six new players to their lineup during the November break, so they're a much improved team from the one we tied 2-2 earlier in the season. The dressing rooms in Cherepovets are below ice level, like the ones in the old Chicago Stadium, where you actually had to climb down a set of stairs – in skates – to get off the ice and climb up a set of stairs to go back on. About halfway through the pre-game warm-up I generally head to the coaching room, which is usually adjacent to the dressing room, to prepare for our final brief meeting just before game time. In

Cherepovets I walked down the stairs to the coach's room, but as I got my final notes completed I noticed there were no other coaches around. I walked down the hall to the dressing room and there were no players there either. I looked at my watch; the warm-up was definitely over and the game was supposed to start in less than fifteen minutes. Where was everybody?

Suddenly I heard a voice calling for me. It was Yuri, our equipment manager, hustling down the hallway. Unbeknownst to me, the visitors use a small dressing room upstairs at ice level to avoid the steep set of stairs and long walk down the hallway. So I raced up the hall, up the stairs, and there were the other coaches and players, all sitting in this dressing room wondering where the heck I was.

Happily, it didn't have any effect on the outcome. We won 4-1 and played a smart and complete game. It helped that Travis Scott returned to the net after missing three games and looked good.

December 4

We scheduled a rare day off for players after arriving home at two a.m. from yet another successful road trip. Linda was back from her trip to Cabo San Lucas, Mexico, and I was happy to see her. Spending six days in Magnitogorsk without her last week gave me a sense of how lonely it must be for her when I'm out on the road. The difference is that I get to go to the hockey rink every day and run practice and review videotape. She doesn't have that time commitment. We decided before we came here that she should travel every six weeks or so; otherwise, it would be a long, difficult year for her. One thing about Linda: she's adaptable and is used to spending time on her own. The difference here is that she doesn't have a circle of friends and can't take quilting classes or other hobby classes the way she did elsewhere. She loves to read, has finished knitting a sweater for our granddaughter Victoria, and is currently knitting one for our grandson Daniel. She brought along some quilting projects and spends a lot of time on the computer, typing up my notes for this book and keeping us in touch with the rest of the world. We do a newsletter for our friends in North America and Europe as well. And it's amazing what she can whip up in our small kitchen. She often comments on how easy it is to live in North America with our big fridges and ovens as well as all the convenient small appliances. Here our kitchen is stocked with the bare-bones basics: four of each utensil, plus four dinner plates, side plates, and bowls. We thought we might buy more, but when you have to hand-wash everything, we figured we could get by with the minimum. We also bought a bread machine since we find the bread here is often stale. It sits on shelves in the stores but isn't covered in plastic, so we just prefer to bake our own.

December 5

Today, on my run along the river behind the arena, I came across a stray female dog with two six-week old puppies huddled in a cardboard box that used to hold a television set. Someone had turned the box on its side and put some straw on the ground to create a makeshift doghouse. This just broke my heart. Linda and I are both dog lovers, so we hustled up to the grocery store to buy some milk and dog food. We rushed back down to the river and instantly fell in love with the puppies and their scrawny, half-starved mother. She barked at us at first, but quickly realized that we were there to help. By the time we were ready to leave, she was letting us pick up her babies. You could tell by their body language that they weren't used to humans, and they made little moaning noises the whole time they were being held. They'd been surviving on only their mother's milk, so they didn't seem too interested in the food, but their mother inhaled it like a Hoover vacuum cleaner. We also brought down a towel and pillow to put in the bottom of the cardboard box, as the temperatures are now dropping to minus ten or twelve at night. We named the pups Seibu (puck) and Klutchka (stick).

December 6

Before practice I ran over and fed the dogs, whose appetites simply amazed me. The mother really needs the food to keep up her strength and milk supply for the pups. We went back to feed them again in the afternoon, and on the way to the store we found an old carpet that someone had slung over the edge of a garbage container. We felt like two homeless people as we grabbed it and took it down to cover the top of the box and give their little family more protection from the cold. We now have a new focus and I can tell that we'll be spending a lot of money on dog food and milk.

December 7

We're feeding our dogs twice a day now – and thinking of them as "our dogs" – and only wish we could bring them home to our apartment. Unfortunately, we live on the eighth floor and travel so much that it isn't practical. But we brought our translator to the area where the dogs live and he talked to a security guard and his wife, who were aware of the situation. We wanted to find out if they thought it would be all right to take the puppies away from their mom so they could be sold at the big outdoor market. We'd pay to have a veterinarian examine the pups and give them their shots. As parents ourselves, we hate the idea of taking the puppies away from their mother, but practically speaking they're a burden on her and it's only going to get colder. Plus they'll just become two more homeless dogs who won't have enough to eat and could possibly be killed by traffic.

December 9

The latest rumours suggest that Molot Perm, the last-place team beset by so many problems, may fold. They haven't paid their players in months.

The Russian Federation confirmed that Malkin will be required to go to the world junior championships in Vancouver, meaning that he'll be playing a lot of hockey in the next month.

Tonight we played Khimik for the first time since they added all those reinforcements from Lada. It was an important game because they're second to us in terms of points gained in the second round of the schedule. We won 4-1, making it ten victories in a row. The mood is ebullient in our dressing room for a lot of reasons, including the fact that the players earn bonus money for every victory, so they have a collective vested financial interest in our success.

When I first heard about this system, I wondered how it would work out. In the last game we actually lost, to Red Army back in early October, one of my young defencemen, Evgeny Biryukov, pinched late in the game and got beat; they scored and we lost. I worried about how this would be received in the dressing room, since Biryukov's mistake took money out of the players' pockets. But nothing was said. It's amazing how the players understood that it could have just as easily happened to them. I was really impressed by the response – or the lack thereof. In Russia the players don't get individual bonuses, it's all team bonuses. If we win, even if a player isn't dressed, it's money in the bank for everybody. So when a guy's not playing, he may not be happy, but when we win, he's thinking, It's not too bad. We have sixty-one points now, so everybody's made an extra $25,000 or so in bonuses.

We've lost only three games – and in the new playoff system, where sixteen teams qualify instead of just eight, finishing first would help us get a favourable playoff matchup. We'd play the sixteenth seeded team; it doesn't matter where they're located. There's no concern here about geography. In fact, even though there's so much at stake in the playoffs, the way we prepare for them is really not very good.

Over here they sacrifice everything for the Olympic Games. And our schedule is so interrupted. We've already had one national team break in November; we play ten games, then break next week for the Rosno Cup, another international competition. We're also going to play in the Spengler Cup, and had to change two league games to accommodate our participation. Then we'll come back and play until January, after which we'll get a thirty-day break. Think about that – a thirty-day break before the final week of the season. Whatever momentum you might have built up over the first forty-six games of the season could disappear in the final five. I've never heard of anything quite like it.

The win over Khimik, which followed a convincing 5-0 win over Avangard Omsk two days before, was our last game before the break for the Rosno Cup, so in the VIP room after the game there was much rejoicing and toasts. The word *Spabearday* was used for every toast. It means victory – and we've had more than our share of late.

December 10

With four days off and not enough time to slip away to Germany or elsewhere, Linda and I are off to Moscow for a few days of sightseeing and Christmas shopping, just to get a break from the tediousness of Magnitogorsk. We're into the dark days of the winter. It's cold. It's drab. That steel plant bellows out smoke every morning. I like to sleep with our windows open and recently, at about four o'clock in the morning, the smell of that coal dust was so strong that we had to close the windows. We suspect that at night, under cover of darkness, the steel plant expels the most toxins in the air. We're upwind from the plant, which is good. The prevailing wind tends to blow in the other direction, so only on the odd day do we get the wind coming our way. I can't believe there are people who live on the other side of the Ural River, downwind from the plant. It's like the Third World there. You'd be shocked at how people can live in those apartments and at how much pollution just hangs above them, all day, every day. It's unbelievable.

When I used to run in the mornings, every day I'd see the same two or three homeless people down the road by the arena. They've got their sacks with all their possessions with them. I don't know where they hunker down for the night, or why they go down to the river, because that's the coldest place. I can only assume it's because there are trees, there's privacy, and no one bothers them.

I don't think you see any homeless people in Canada close to the ones here. They're filthy. They're already ill. And they're already completely gone in the morning on alcohol. In our building the ground-level apartments have these little open alcoves on their foundations, and that's where some of these people sleep. They've got old cardboard boxes they found in a garbage dump and I don't know how they're going to survive the cold nights. My interpreter tells me there's a homeless shelter here, but I've never seen it. I should ask him to show it to me. These people don't appear to have any place to go. I mean, there's a homeless problem wherever you go in the world, but this is far grimmer than anything I've seen. The safety net in Canada or in the U.S. or in places in Europe doesn't seem to exist here – and it's mostly older people.

In the shift towards capitalism, the pensions of these older people just got destroyed by inflation. It's sad to see how some of them have to supplement their incomes. Every day you see these old ladies, down on every street corner, with their little table and a stool. On the table they have jars of preserves – stewed beets, or jams, or honey, or some vegetables they're trying to sell, or garlic rings hanging from sticks. It's pathetic. Kids with Kool-Aid stands look better than this. It's cold and they're there all day – old ladies and old men, in their seventies and eighties, trying to eke out a living, selling produce or whatever they can get their hands on to supplement their meagre pensions. Down close to the market, sometimes people will set up a table selling used gadgets, things that we'd throw in the garbage. But they have to make a living.

The oligarchs have been criticized for having no social conscience, which is why Putin's really coming down hard on some of them. He's saying that they have to do things for the people; that they have to put money back into the country and can't just take and take and take. That's why the oligarchs are involved in sport – and Putin has other initiatives that he wants them involved in as well. They're not doing it on their own. They're being told they have to do it. He's forcing them to put money into some social structures, but it's slow going by the looks of things.

December 11

Today the final transfer window of the season opens. It's our version of the NHL trading deadline, the last chance to modify our roster before the December 20 freeze. I'm interested in recruiting Anders Eriksson, a Swede who's currently playing in the minors in North America. We probably need one more defenceman to strengthen our depth at that position, so we're talking to him and to Karel Pilar, an ex-Toronto Maple Leaf defenceman. Overall, though, it doesn't look as if the market for North American players will be very good. We may have to go with the team we've got, which I don't mind. That's actually good for us. We're in good shape. The teams chasing us are the ones that have work to do.

For us, the focus remains mainly on the world junior. For all the great players they continue to develop, Russia hasn't had a lot of success internationally in recent years, so there's pressure on the federation to turn that around. Obviously they'd be a much better team with Malkin, which is why the national junior coach is politicking big-time with the federation to get him. To me, what's interesting is that he also coaches Ufa, one of the better teams in our league. So I question his motives. I wonder, Why do you really want Malkin so badly? To play him about fifty-eight minutes a game so there's nothing left of him for our league's playoffs? And Krikunov, who coaches Dynamo, will probably play Malkin's butt off at the Olympics too.

In my worst nightmares I have a vision of this scrawny kid coming back to our team in early March, wasted because he's played so much. It's as though they'll take a racehorse and run him too hard. You can't push a racehorse too far or you'll break the horse. The same can happen with an elite-level athlete – everybody's just going to take their pound of flesh out of this kid and break him down.

December 12

Leaving for Moscow today, Linda and I are on the same flight as Travis Scott, Igor Korolev, and Dmitri Yushkevich, who are all making the trek back to North America for whirlwind visits with their families. We're going literally to play tourist. I saw a lot of the sights during my visits to Moscow with Team Canada, but Linda wasn't with me – and besides, a lot has changed. We're accompanied by Igor, my translator, who's been invaluable to me. Igor was working for MMK in the main offices as a travel coordinator and host for visiting foreign executives who came to Magnitogorsk to tour the steel mill. Up until now, his role with the hockey team was limited to accompanying them to various European Cup tournaments because of his language skills. When they hired me to coach, Igor joined the team on a full-time basis. He's as much a babysitter for Linda and me as he is a translator. He helps with the shopping and the banking. He calls us our taxis and generally helps troubleshoot the day-to-day issues that come up. Without him at press conferences, I'd be lost.

When we travel, Igor always sits beside me on the plane and feeds me interesting facts about the cities we're visiting. He's a well-educated intellectual and a diehard hockey fan, making him a great companion when we go for walks on the road. Before every game he's taken to writing down a predicted score inside his cigarette package – and it's amazing how often he's right. Almost every day Linda and I make the same declaration – Thank God we have Igor. Jokingly, she calls him her Russian husband.

Besides having Igor along today, the team arranged for Roman, our Moscow liaison, to pick us up at the airport and drive us around to do our sightseeing. Our first stop is the Kremlin in downtown Moscow, where we visit a museum that houses artifacts from the days of the czars. Linda is blown away by the display of ornate coaches and sleighs that were once used to drive the nobility around. No wonder they had a revolution. Naturally, we also visited Lenin's tomb, where the lines are as long as they were twenty years ago. The rules are the same too. First we had to pass through a metal detector, and then we paid to store our cameras since they still don't allow you to take any pictures.

The next day we visited a military museum, whose exhibits feature several of the key Russian battles that affected the outcome of World War II. It was snowing quite heavily and a large parking lot close by was basically empty, but we were told we can't park there because it's not meant for visitors. Of course, that didn't deter Roman. He pulled right up to a guard shack, slipped the guy 150 rubles, and suddenly up goes the gate and in we go.

Like so many places in Russia, a little money can change the rules quickly. There's a story we've been told about an airline disaster in the summer of 2004, where two domestic flights crashed within minutes of each other. The investigation later proved that security people were bribed to let two women get on the planes without submitting their carry-on luggage to X-rays. Seeing how easily we've just entered an off-limits parking lot makes you realize how these things can happen.

Bribery remains a way of life here. Russians often say that a new building may cost US$40 to $50 million for the construction, but that with kickbacks and bribes it may cost $5 to $10 million more. Igor told us a famous Russian joke that says it all for Muscovites. A businessman is trying to get some political favours from a politician, so he offers him twenty thousand rubles and explains that no one needs to know about his involvement. The politician replies, "Give me fifty thousand rubles and we'll tell everybody."

We rode the subway, we visited the Gum department store, and we stocked up on groceries and goods we can't get in Magnitogorsk. We also visited the Moscow Circus and the Bolshoi Ballet. For dinners, we'd indulge in hamburgers and ribs to get a taste of North America. These are foods we can't find in Magnitogorsk, and since we don't have a barbeque, we can't cook them for ourselves either. On our final day, a Sunday, the four of us attended St. Basil's

Church, a famous landmark that was closed for services during the Communist regime. This church has a special meaning for me because one of my all-time favourite photographs is of my son Andy standing in front of it.

Andy was with me in 1987, in the pre-Olympic year, when we came over here to play the prestigious Izvestia tournament. We had Sean Burke in goal, Zarley Zalapski and Randy Gregg anchoring our defence, and Marc Habscheid, the current national team coach, as one of our forwards. We were the heavy underdogs – no Canadian team had won so much as a single game on Russian soil since the 1972 Summit Series. Those were also the final days of the Soviet hockey machine: they had Fetisov and Kasatonov on defence and Larionov, Krutov, and Makarov up front. It was classic David versus Goliath, and this time David won. Four months after, the '87 Team Canada of Gretzky, Lemieux, and Larry Murphy won the Canada Cup in three hard-fought matches, all of which ended with the same 6-5 score; we upset basically the same Russian team on their own turf. It was a magical moment, but it flew under the radar screen back home in Canada since there was no television coverage of the event.

Ultimately, though, it may have undermined our chances four months later at the 1988 Olympics in Calgary (where *Sports Illustrated* picked us to win the gold medal in what would have been a monumental upset) because it put the Soviets on guard. There was no way we could sneak up on them the way the Americans did in the 1980 Miracle on Ice. By the time the Soviets got to Calgary they were on top of their game, and we couldn't duplicate our Izvestia success in the Olympics. Still, that was a memorable moment in my coaching career. Last year, at the world championships in Vienna, I sat with Victor Tikhonov and his son (who coached briefly in the San Jose Sharks organization) and asked him which he considered the best team he ever coached. He answered, "The 1987-88 team."

December 17

Ah, Russia. A day after it looked as if Molot would almost certainly not survive, they arranged a US$1 million bank loan that will cover their expenses for the rest of the season. The only problem was that, because the players hadn't been paid in so long and it looked as if the team would fold imminently, a dozen of their players had already declared their contracts void, signed new deals with other teams, and left. So two days ago Molot had players but no money, and today they have money but no players. In order to finish the season, Molot will now have to do what Lada did earlier this season and pick up a dozen players from the lower league or borrow young players from other Super League teams. I'm beginning to learn something about the economics of Russian hockey – or more precisely, its business model. Essentially, there is none. Every team operates in the red.

In the NHL, gate receipts account for the largest part of a team's gross revenue. That isn't the case in Russia. Gate receipts are negligible. It costs anywhere from two to seven dollars tops to go to a game, depending on where you are and where you happen to sit. But it's cheap. In time, that could go up as people get more affluent, but I don't think more than 5 to 10 per cent of a team's budget comes out of gate receipts. It's minimal. There's also no TV money. Yet they want to televise the games because it helps them attract sponsors; they can tell potential sponsors that their board advertisement will be on television.

Ninety per cent of the revenue comes from either advertising or sponsorship. Our sweaters have sponsors' logos on them. They're also heavily into board advertising, something the NHL actually borrowed from the European leagues. But mostly, every team has a major sponsor that underwrites its costs in any given year. Sometimes the major sponsor can be a person or the person's company. Dynamo has people who put money in privately. Some teams even have government sponsors. In Ufa, for example, their building is provided to them, free of charge, by the government. They don't pay rent on it. In other places it's the same arrangement – the regional government provides funding because they want the team; it gives that region, or city, an identity. Luxury seating is coming in with all the new buildings, but even it isn't necessarily used as a cash cow, but rather as a vehicle to attract sponsors and advertisers.

Compared with the NHL, the economic model makes no sense. The teams all lose money. In the NHL, some teams may lose money, but the goal is to operate in the black, which of course is why they had the lockout. They don't want to lose money in Russia either, but they just know they will. There's no viable business model. It may eventually come into the twenty-first century, but from the Molot example and others, that looks to be a long way away. As for our team, Rashnikov thinks it builds identification within Magnitogorsk and brings attention to the city nationally and internationally. But it's a loss leader. He puts money into it – and he doesn't get any back.

December 19

We don't live in a great neighbourhood, even by Magnitogorsk standards. Its primary appeal is the fact that the rink is within walking distance; we can actually see it from our balcony. But we come across a lot of conspicuous poverty every day, and Linda and I often talk about what we can do to make a difference while we're here. Our travel agent told Linda that there are three orphanages in Magnitogorsk. Some kids have actually lost their parents. Mostly, though, they're the children of alcoholics or drug addicts or parents who are too poor to care for them. Only one of the orphanages is subsidized by MMK, so we decided to see if, in conjunction with the players, we could do something to help one of the unsubsidized orphanages. The players agreed to contribute some of their earnings to help buy Christmas presents for the kids. They also gave us permission to raid the "fine" fund they pay into whenever they're guilty of a minor transgression and turn that over to the orphanage as well.

The orphanage has seventy-eight children, who have been divided into six families. Every family has a group "mother" who administers to her own "children." Two of these mothers accompanied Igor and Linda to buy gifts for the orphanage and for the children. They visited electronic stores and department stores and bought ping-pong sets, badminton sets, hockey sticks, dolls, toy cars and trucks, skipping ropes, and other articles from the outdoor market. Everything was taken back to the orphanage and hidden away until December 24, when the plan is for Linda and me, plus a handful of players, along with Timothei the fox, the team mascot, to play Santa and distribute the toys.

The orphanage also has a pet cat, which made me think that our adopted pups were about eight weeks old now. We didn't want to leave them with their mother for too much longer. They were starting to eat solid food, and if we don't keep feeding them we're worried that they might die or get killed by a car or truck. So we asked Igor to ask Julia, the orphanage director, if they might be interested in having some puppies. She immediately said yes, so later that day we brought the puppies to the orphanage, where they were adopted by two of the surrogate mothers. We felt terrible about taking the pups away from their mother, but it's been getting colder and snowing more, and this was a better alternative.

December 20

The team was supposed to fly to Moscow today to play MVD in Tver, but it was foggy when we woke up and the fog didn't lift all day, so we can't leave until tomorrow. In the meantime we did our last bit of recruiting for the season, signing Swedish defenceman Anders Eriksson to a contract. Eriksson played four hundred-plus NHL games with Detroit, Chicago, Florida, Toronto, and Columbus, but has been in the American League all year. He's our third and final import of the season (Travis Scott and Igor Vorobiev are the others) and will add depth to our power play.

Because we couldn't travel today, I was home having lunch with Linda when all of a sudden we heard a big commotion outside our apartment building. Cars and buses pulled up outside and a crowd of people appeared, all dressed in black and milling around behind our apartment complex. I said to Linda, "What could this possibly be, a protest or something?" It turned out to be a funeral – or more precisely, a visitation in advance of a funeral. As we were watching out the window, two men carried out a great flat coffin and put it on four stools in the courtyard. They adjusted the deceased man's tie and all the mourners took turns paying their respects. Then they had a little procession out from the back of our common area, through our gate, and then to the front parking lot. Instead of a hearse, they put the man in a van and left the coffin uncovered. All the cars and buses pulled out in a cavalcade, and off they went to the cemetery. Later, we learned the significance of this odd ceremony – that in Russia it's customary for the deceased to be brought back to say goodbye to their home.

December 21

The good news: the fog lifted, so we were able to catch the scheduled Magnitogorsk-Moscow flight. The bad news: we were late arriving because of a serious snowstorm. Our planned ninety-minute bus ride to Tver took more than four-and-a-half hours, as the roads were jammed with traffic and the going was slow. We arrived at the arena at 5:45 for a seven o'clock game. The players were hungry and tired, but somehow we found a way to win 3-1.

Malkin was back with us after playing in the Rosno Cup, but this was to be his last game until January 10. He leaves tomorrow for Canada and the world junior tournament, so we'll have to tackle the Spengler Cup competition by ourselves, without our best player and most prolific scorer.

Dave and Linda King at St. Basil's Cathedral
in Moscow's Red Square.

PART 3 **WINTER**

December 22

I TURNED FIFTY-EIGHT TODAY AND celebrated my birthday in the Moscow suburb of Chekhov, where we'll play Vityaz tomorrow in our final game before the Spengler Cup. It isn't the first time I've spent my birthday in Russia – on the day I turned forty, I celebrated what was probably one of the sweetest victories of my career at the Izvestia tournament, against the Soviet national team of Larionov, Fetisov, and all the rest of their great players. In those days I'd always get home just in time for Christmas. That won't happen this year. I'm part of the landscape now.

I started coaching the year I turned twenty-five, and it's natural, on your birthday, to ruminate about past experiences. The older you get, the more you think you've seen it all – and then a year like this one comes along and you realize there's a lot left to see, learn, and absorb.

People sometimes ask me how my approach differs from when I started off behind the bench of the Billings Bighorns almost thirty years ago. My answer is that, after so many years of coaching, I've come to understand more and more about the players' side of the game. As a young coach you often watch in frustration from the bench and wonder why a guy couldn't make the right play. The longer you coach, the more you realize that observing from the bench and playing on the ice can be two very, very different things. The players are in the midst of the game, with all the action swirling around them. I'm watching from the outside, looking in. From the bench, I can see their options. On the ice, because they're being pressured, they can't always see those options, so they sometimes make the wrong choices. You learn to say to yourself, I can show him a couple of things tomorrow in training, or I can show him a video clip of that, or I can catch him as he skates off the ice and show him on the board how to fix that.

As you get older, your timing as a coach is also much better. You know when to give feedback and you know when to shut up. That, to me, is really critical. When you're young, you're just so impetuous. You want to correct things immediately, even if your timing, in terms of providing useful feedback, is wrong.

My relationship with players over the years has been mixed. Some of the guys who've played for me are my closest friends in the game; with others, we didn't see eye to eye. But today was something quite unique. At every turn I was made to feel warmly, unexpectedly welcome. The Russian government sent me a congratulatory telegram. The owner of the Vityaz team sent me a bottle of Veuve Cliquot champagne. But the best moment of all came at our team's pre-game supper. There I was, sitting at my table, and suddenly, out of nowhere, a pizza is delivered to my place. Somehow in the last few months they've absorbed the fact that I'm a pizza junkie. It told me that the players clearly knew something about me as a person, and not just as a hockey coach. It was a thoughtful gesture and touched me a great deal. They also had a couple of gifts for me – a tie and a watch – and then they sang Happy Birthday in English. They went to a lot of trouble on my behalf, on a day when they were taxed to the limit by the travel and the schedule. I was impressed. It was nice. It was something I'll remember for a long time.

December 24

On Christmas Eve we're back in Magnitogorsk after a 2-1 OT victory over Vityaz. The team will get the day off before we leave for Davos, but before we take off we have an appointment at the orphanage to distribute gifts. Traditionally, Christmas Day is celebrated on January 7 in Russia, but the holiday is slowly evolving and the 25th of December is starting to take on a new importance. Many stores have their Christmas lights up already. There's even a giant decorated tree in front of City Hall.

A lot of the children in the orphanage are Metallurg hockey fans, so they were excited to see which players would come. Sadly, Malkin couldn't be there, because he's in Canada right now, but Igor Korolev, Evgeny Gladskikh, Alexei Kaigorodov, Ravil Gusmanov, and Dmitri Pestunov all showed up. The children prepared an entertainment program for us, singing and dancing. They were so excited that the players came to visit. And naturally, the team mascot was a huge hit with the kids. It was gratifying to see how well our players represented the team. We took turns handing out presents and then the kids dispersed to their large communal rooms to open their packages and play with their gifts. Our Russian isn't good enough yet to carry on a conversation, but the smiles on the children's faces and their obvious delight spoke volumes. We were impressed with the love the orphanage staff showed to the children and left there with promises to return soon.

In February we're planning to go to Calgary for a one-week mini-holiday. After telling our son Andy and his wife, Sara, about the orphanage, they decided to purchase some new clothing for the children and to scour their house for clothing our grandchildren have outgrown. When we asked the orphanage if there was anything else we could do, they told us they'd like to acquire six samovars so that they can re-establish the Russian tradition of having tea at night with their "families."

December 25

Christmas Day – and for the first time in our thirty-four-year marriage, Linda and I didn't put up a tree, wrap any presents, or decorate our home. Instead, we're taking a few gifts to Davos for Andy's and Scott's families, but we decided against exchanging presents. Instead, we'll donate the money we'd normally spend on each other to the orphanage.

Our plane, an old Soviet jet that flew us directly from Magnitogorsk to Zurich, was jam-packed. Most of the players brought their wives or girlfriends and children with them. Anders Eriksson and his wife, Beth, joined us at the airport; he'll make his debut for us at the Spengler Cup. From Zurich we took a bus up to Davos, where we'll open the tournament tomorrow against Canada. I can't begin to tell you how odd and unsettled that will make me feel. I didn't just coach the Canadian national team for nine years; I was one of a group of people, along with Bill Hay and Father David Bauer, who were instrumental in bringing back to Canada a full-time national team. I had a lot of input into that program, so for me and my family, our hearts are and always will be with that team. I'm going to find it awkward to coach against them and have my family in the stands, my grandchildren wearing their little Magnitogorsk jerseys, cheering for a Russian team against Canada. This, in a roundabout way, allows us to come full circle. Twice in the early 1980s I spent Christmas apart from my wife and children, and as a result I decided to not let that happen again. After that my family joined me in Davos on three occasions (in 1985, 1989, and 1990) so we were able to enjoy both Christmas and the Spengler Cup together.

Andy and his family had already arrived in Davos, so when we got to the hotel we called up to their room; a few minutes later our grandchildren, Victoria and Daniel, came tearing across the lobby and gave us great big hugs. I haven't seen them since early July, when I left for Russia. Victoria and Daniel are staying in our hotel with us, so after a nice Christmas meal with the team and their families we went up to our room with Andy and Sara and exchanged small gifts.

December 26

I'd been in touch with Marc Habscheid, who now coaches Team Canada, in the weeks leading up to the Spengler Cup. He'll be part of Pat Quinn's coaching staff at the Olympics in Turin and he wanted to get a scouting report on some of the international referees they'll see in Italy. He also warned that he had some tricks up his sleeve and planned to play them on me once the tournament got underway. When Habby played for me, he and Randy Gregg were the two biggest practical jokers on the team, so I was trying to anticipate what he might do. Would he call a stick measurement against us? Or maybe cut my stick almost all the way through with a handsaw, so that when you take one shot it breaks? He's done that before.

Or would he sneak in and put water in my skates like he did in the 1987-88 pre-Olympic year, when we were practising at a really cold rink in Grindalwald, Switzerland? We were there to do some training and the guys wanted a day off, so they thought that if they put a little water in my skates, I might agree to it – because who wants to practise in a freezing-cold rink in wet skates?

In those days, I had these Micron skates that came with the liners. So Habby snuck in, pulled the liners out, and soaked them in water. It was almost straight out of one of those Bobby Orr commercials you see on TV, where the kids are playing a trick on Bobby and giggling outside the dressing room. Except I'm not real happy with this and I thought, No way are they going to get to me. This is a battle of wills. So out I go. I walked through the dressing room and you could hear my skates go squish, squish with every step I took. I knew all the guys were watching too, so I didn't even blink as I walked by them all. I was the first one on the ice and I could sense them thinking, Uh-oh, we're in for a long day now because Kinger's pissed. I wasn't going to let them get away it. I found out later that Habby, Wally Schreiber, and Randy Gregg were all in on the joke.

Randy and Habby had the most fun that year playing tricks on people. When we'd wait in airports, they'd take coins and glue them to the floor. People would walk by, see a coin lying there, and try to pick it up, and of course they couldn't. The players would be sitting nearby, trying to keep a straight face, but eventually they'd be howling with laughter. Or sometimes they'd attach a five-dollar bill to the end of a fishing line and lay it on the floor. When people stooped to pick it up, they'd give it a little jerk so that it was always just out of reach. They'd do it again and again, and sometimes the poor sucker – stooped over – would chase this thing for ten or twenty feet before finally realizing he'd been had. It was *Candid Camera* without the camera – and nowadays, probably, they'd be recording it all for posterity on their camera phones. They'd do all those things to lighten the mood on a long travel day and it kept the team loose. It was great harmless fun.

But today, preparing for our game, Marc seemed really tight beforehand, I don't know why. They outplayed us by a wide margin too, but we managed to get the game to a shootout, and ultimately won 2-1. Our team wasn't very good, but our Canadian goalie, Travis Scott, was exceptional – and the irony of that didn't escape anyone in the building; that a Canadian playing for a Russian team almost single-handedly beat Team Canada.

Afterwards Linda and I celebrated our thirty-fifth wedding anniversary, and the best I could do for her was get us a win. Not every wife would appreciate that, but she does. Almost through our entire marriage I've coached a game on our anniversary, so she's used to it.

December 27

Our game against Canada didn't end until around eleven o'clock last night, and today we were back on the ice for a game at three in the afternoon to play against Pierre Page's Berlin Eisbaren, last year's DEL champions. The Spengler Cup is a five-team tournament, which means that every team gets one day off in the preliminary round. Unhappily for us, our "bye" day isn't until the fifth day, meaning we play four games in four days, which is a tremendously taxing amount of hockey.

I knew we were at altitude and that we had a long flight to get here, but I sensed we had no edge at all to our play. Our guys were just going through the motions. Halfway through the game, I said to myself, This isn't going to work – I have to get in front of these guys and look them right in the face. So I did something that I hadn't done before, but something they'd understand right away. I coached the rest of the game from the front of the bench, the way the Russians usually do, so that I could talk to the guys directly and they could see my energy and hopefully feed off me. I got much more demonstrative – and the team suddenly recognized that they needed to pick up their intensity. As a coach, you have to read your team, and I just felt that if I didn't get in front of them we'd go nowhere. Even though we were inconsistent again, we won 4-3 in a shootout. Konstantin Simchuk got the start in goal and he was outstanding in the shootout.

December 28

The fatigue caught up to us today in our third game in three days against the host team HC Davos. Davos added seven players to its roster for the tournament – four Finns, two Americans, and one

Canadian – and they played great, beating us 4-1. We looked tired and out of sync. I'm not optimistic about our chances the rest of the way.

December 30

We finally got a day off today, after somehow beating Sparta Prague 4-3 yesterday. Our record – one regulation win, two shootout wins, and a loss, good for seven points – probably isn't going to get us into the two-team final. Today's afternoon game between Canada and Sparta Prague doesn't affect our playoff chances, but the evening game, Berlin versus HC Davos, does. Berlin is out already but Davos, the host team, desperately wants to win their own tournament and defend the title they won last year. For us to qualify for the final, Berlin needs to knock off Davos, which nobody thinks is going to happen – except, of course, that it does. They won 8-5, meaning that our seven points was good enough for second place and that now we'll play a rematch against Canada in the final tomorrow at noon.

Since no one expected this result, a lot of our players were out for the evening with their families. By the time we got in touch with everybody, it was late, real late. I hastily made up a schedule for tomorrow and asked the team to gather at seven-thirty in the morning for breakfast so that we can get out of bed, eat, and get moving.

December 31

Unbeknownst to me, the team breakfast was accidentally left off the schedule posted for the players in the hotel lobby, so when I arrived for breakfast after my run, I was there all by myself. I went back to look at the schedule in the lobby and sure enough, there was no pre-game breakfast listed, so now I was concerned. The players would arrive for a nine-thirty video meeting and may or may not have had anything to eat before departing for the arena at ten o'clock. This is not the way to prepare for a tournament final.

Just before puck drop I saw my old friend Habby again, and he was looking so serious. They'd had a great tournament after losing the first game to us, but you'd never know it from that hangdog look on his face. So I thought, I've got to go over and take a little pressure off him. It used to work the other way. When I coached him, I was the guy with the worried look on my face and he was the happy guy. I tried to lighten him up and I don't know if it worked because, improbably, we played our best game of the tournament, won 8-3, and somehow emerged as tournament champions.

The truth is, I felt bad for Team Canada when it was over because they were the best team overall in the tournament. I just loved watching them play – they were smart and disciplined. Even though I was coaching the other team, I was so proud of the way Canada played. Against us, we got up 6-2 and it could have gotten ugly, but it didn't. They were a class act all the way.

At the end of the medal presentation, my grandchildren Daniel and Victoria took turns wearing my medal, and were so excited. I gave it to them so that they could to take it home to Canada for me. Victoria carefully packed it in her backpack; she'd already told her parents that she wanted to take it to school for show and tell. Daniel kept telling us that he was coming to Russia with his grandpa for a sleepover.

Afterwards I got to thinking about how this win might be good for our team long-term. We were less dynamic at the Spengler Cup without Malkin, but still effective in many ways. Any time you play without your top player, it's a chance to see your team in a different light. I liked seeing the players grind it out and have to win a different way. We weren't as spectacular without Malkin, but we played reasonably well. Three or four guys who hadn't been playing very much were suddenly getting lots of playing time, and they made the most of it. In hindsight, winning the tournament without Malkin might be the best thing that ever happened to us because it showed our players that we didn't necessarily need him to win.

We also won without our normal preparation, and that was not the way I like it. The Spengler Cup is more like a hockey festival than a hockey tournament. So the players' edge or intensity wasn't where you wanted it to be. At our pre-game meals there were sixty people, not twenty. There were guys with their kids, cutting their food for them. It wasn't an insulated situation any more. There were so many things that would give you an excuse not to win – and we won. There was so much you couldn't control that you'd like to control – but we won. I kept saying, "We want to win it, but how badly do we want to win it?" I didn't know. It just seemed odd that we'd be so successful under not-close-to-perfect circumstances for the coaching staff and for the players. I learned something from it. Sometimes, you don't sweat the little things.

I was all for a low-key celebration but Velichkin, our GM, would have none of that. He said we'd celebrate the New Year's win three times – on Magnitogorsk time first, because that's the earliest, then on Moscow time, then on Davos time. Clearly, they love New Year's in Russia. They embrace it far more than they do Christmas. And to celebrate it with my new Russian friends proved to be so interesting because they're such fun people. They're loud. They're boisterous. They cheer. I'm more subdued. I stayed for Magnitogorsk New Year's and Moscow New Year's, but then I could sense it was time to let the players have some time on their own. I don't watch them, but I think they think I do. So I left the players on their own to have a good time.

January 1, 2006

Last night's party spilled into the wee small hours, so many of our people were dealing with the after-effects as we made our way to the Zurich airport for a three p.m. charter flight home – a disaster from start to finish. Somehow the paperwork required for refuelling the plane had been overlooked, so it took time to address that problem. Then they discovered that the paperwork for arranging our airline meals had also been forgotten, so we ended up flying home with no food on board.

The smokers in our management group – and there are lots of them – decided to turn the galley into a smoking lounge and spent the entire five-hour flight smoking and toasting each other with the Swiss liquor they brought onboard. I was annoyed by that and annoyed even further when, upon arriving back in the Big M, as Linda and I now call Magnitogorsk, we were greeted by a team of security people. For the first time in my long flying career, all our luggage had to be X-rayed coming off the flight. Why was today different from any other day? No one can say. They just shrug. This is Russia; eventually you learn to stop asking questions.

January 3

Now that we're back from Switzerland, we've discovered what a big hit we were when we were away, not just in Magnitogorsk, but all across Russia. Moscow, for example, has two oversized TV screens in the downtown, and on New Year's Eve they had to close off two streets because so many people stopped to watch our Spengler Cup win on the big screen that it got to be a safety issue. Even though we were Magnitogorsk, a club team, we were Team Russia at the Spengler Cup. Because this tournament is so well marketed in

Europe, it's become a major event. I didn't realize that. Every day since we've been back they've replayed the game on television in Magnitogorsk. By the looks of it, they just aren't going to let this one go any time soon.

January 4

After practice, our players watched Russia play the U.S. at the world junior championships in Vancouver. Malkin was really good in that game and the Russians won convincingly, setting up a Canada-Russia final, in which the Russians are favoured to win.

January 5

What a surprise. Canada didn't just win the world junior; they overwhelmed the Russians 5-0 in the final game. Malkin was shut out, while Anton Khudobin, a nineteen-year-old goaltender from Magnitogorsk who's playing for the Saskatoon Blades of the Western League this season, got shelled in net. I decided to keep a low profile. I felt bad for the three players from our team who played so well right up until the final and I don't want them coming back to hear I was gloating or otherwise celebrating Canada's victory.

The Russians got a pretty good tournament out of Nikolai Kulemin, who played on Malkin's line in the world junior tournament. He wasn't much of a factor on our team in the first half, playing only about seventeen of our first thirty-five games, but he'll play the rest of the way. After the November break I started to play him a little more and recognized that he could make us better.

Kulemin is an '86-born and hasn't received much attention until now. I always had the sense that our organization viewed him as a role player. I see something completely different. I like his size and his speed, but mostly I like his game sense, something that a lot of older, more experienced Russian players don't have. He reads off his teammates so well that he's always providing defensive support if someone else is jumping into the attack. His skill level is high enough to play with Malkin, which makes them perfect as linemates: Malkin should take the risks he does to generate offence, and yet it rarely causes us a problem because Nikolai is providing backup.

The NHL's Central Scouting bureau has Kulemin rated extremely low, but I wonder if he didn't catch some eyes at the world juniors. In my view, he'll become a very complete and consistent two-way NHL player. Every day he's the first one on the ice with a pail of pucks and then the last one off, picking up the pucks. He's quiet and polite off the ice, but plays a physical style on the ice. There's tempo and flare to his game, which doesn't necessarily reflect his personality. Somebody's going to get a good one in Kulemin.

January 6

More problems with our strength coach, Viktor Gudzik, today: we had to have a coach's meeting in Moscow to clarify our channels of communication with the players because Gudzik is confusing them. The other day he told them that we'll be stepping up the pace of our off-ice workouts but cutting down our time on the ice. This, of course, is nonsense – not something we've discussed, or want to do. Gudzik, I'm learning, is a desperately insecure man who wants the players to think he's second to me in the chain of command. The three on-ice coaches, plus our team doctor, are clearly tired of his act. I can tell that from their body language when I tell Gudzik off – that if there are any changes in the training schedule, I'll decide and announce them.

January 7

I expected that by now we'd have hit a flat spot in our season, one of those times when the blahs just catch up with you. Every team eventually does, even the best ones. Instead, we keep finding ways to win.

After playing five games in six nights we came back from the Spengler Cup a real tired team, and I wondered how we'd react to the resumption of league play. I looked on the computer to see how some of our Spengler Cup opponents did. Sparta Prague and Berlin Eisbaren both lost their first games back. And we were facing the bottom dwellers in the standings, which isn't always an advantage. Sometimes even a well-rested team will take these games too lightly because a key ingredient – respect – is often missing. But even without Malkin, Kulemin, and Evgeny Biryukov, who still aren't back from Vancouver, we've already won our first two games since returning from Switzerland. They weren't picture perfect, but it said a lot about the quality of our team and the character of our players that they found a way to get the job done.

January 9

Today the Russian Super League unveiled the list of players who'll compete in the January 22 All-Star Game, matching teams from the East against teams from the West. The All-Star Game is a relatively new concept here and is based largely on the NHL model. It's a spectacle, they tell me, more about the glitz and the glamour than the hockey. Sounds familiar, right? Altogether, seven of our players were chosen to play – three defencemen (Varlamov, Atyushov, and Yushkevich); three forwards (Kudermetov, Malkin, and Kaigorodov), plus Travis Scott in goal. I'll be coaching the Eastern team with Peter Vorobiev, the Lada coach. Yurzinov and Bilyeletdinov will coach the West.

Our juniors are back in the lineup today, but they're not at their best. Maybe it's just the jet lag, but Malkin, especially, appears to have picked up some bad habits while he was away. It's just one game, so I'm not going to panic, but if he keeps this up we'll need to have a little video session and show him some things he has to do better. But he's very good that way. He's receptive to feedback. He doesn't fight your input.

January 10

Now that there's good snow cover, every day for the last eight or ten days, we've seen five or six horses go up and down our street, sometimes pulling the famous Russian sleigh, the *troika*. Imagine this: on a busy, busy street in the twenty-first century, lined with cars, bumper to bumper – along come these horses, pulling a sleigh. It's like a glimpse into the past. Today when I was out running, a couple of my dogs were missing and I'm worried about what might have happened to them. Gradually, over the course of the past month, our doggie day-care centre has grown. It started with Lady and her two pups Seibu and Klutchka. After we started feeding them every day, another dog, Blackie, started showing up. She was a homeless guard dog for the ski hill that was being torn down. Scruffy was the next one to appear; I used to see him when I went running by the new Russian Orthodox Church. Then I discovered Pegleg, who may have had a piece of glass in his foot; he basically hobbled around on three feet only. As soon as we fed them for the first time, that was it, they would keep coming back for more. That was their home, the area behind the rink where the new one was being built. The potential for an accident on the roads is great – I've seen three or four dead dogs now and several cats – so I'm wondering where my guys went and if they're still around.

I ended up running by the church looking for the dogs, and as I did I saw a fellow standing there, a street person. His coat and pants were covered with hoarfrost, so I knew he'd been sleeping outside. I always carry a little money in my pocket in case I'm getting bread or milk or something. So I went over to him with fifty rubles and said, "Here, take this." He put his hand out, and it was black and filthy. He just reeked. His age could be anywhere from thirty to fifty, I couldn't tell. But he looked nearly frozen – and when I say that, I mean it literally. It was minus twenty-six this morning and I thought, This guy, where did he sleep last night? It just saddens you to your core. Where I run with the dogs there are a couple of wooded areas where the men – homeless and alcoholic – have made lean-tos out of plastic. In the mornings you'll still see the fires smouldering and pairs of boots and legs sticking out the bottom of the lean-tos. I don't know how they survive.

January 11

When Linda and I were walking back from feeding the dogs we came across a gruesome sight in the landfill area behind the rink. I'm assuming someone had stolen a sheep, hung it up by its feet, and slit its throat. Its decapitated head was lying next to its intestines and stomach. They had completely skinned the sheep and left the skin, lying inside out in the snow along with all the blood and hooves, and taken the carcass for food. I know animals are sometimes stolen and butchered, but behind our arena? What next?

January 12

Linda and I are becoming more and more like Russians every day. For example, everywhere we go now, we carry a shopping bag. It's a canvas bag that's nice and strong and you take it with you because maybe today you'll run across something in the food store you haven't seen before. The other day we saw a head of iceberg lettuce for the first time ever, so I snapped it up right away. I couldn't believe it. I was like, Wow, what's this? We found lettuce, we found celery, and I know this is hard to believe, but it was cause for a minor celebration. I don't want to make it sound as if we're hard done by here, because we're not. The stores are full of great groceries, but good produce is rare, especially in the winter. The variety and the amounts have really shrunk.

Here's something else that's different: in the supermarkets you rarely see older people shopping, because the prices are too high. They have to buy things in the open market, where you can barter a little. There may be ten people selling carrots, so they'll say: "Oh, yours are too expensive, I'll go somewhere else." They argue. They get the prices down.

January 13

After practice today I put on my running gear, grabbed my dog-food bag, and wheeled out to where the dogs were and fed them all. As usual, they followed me back to the rink. The players were just leaving to go to the *baza*, so they saw me coming over the snowbank, running with a pack of dogs. I'm telling you, they couldn't believe it. And of course, the dogs saw the players and started barking at them, so there I was, trying to calm them down – the dogs, I mean, not the players. The players were having a good laugh about it. I know they think I'm obsessive because I'm fixated on running every day. Then they see me with all these stray dogs that no one in Russia gives a second thought to and I'm sure they must think, This coach of ours is a different kind of cat.

January 14

It sometimes amazes me just how quiet Russian players are compared with Canadian and American players. At the Spengler Cup it was interesting to hear all the talk coming from the Canadian bench and dressing room, whereas our players will just sit quietly and get dressed, hardly even looking awake as they prepare to do battle. Only when we get the three-minute warning to prepare for our pregame skate do a few voices surface. Generally, our captain, Evgeny Varlamov, will say the same few things he says before every game. It's no different on the bench or between periods either – deathly silent, with only a few players providing any vocal support or encouragement.

I've learned over time that this isn't unusual; it's the Russian way. The players rarely ever complain or give you any emotional reaction. You might decide upon a shorter practice and advise them of this, and there's no reaction. You might have a longer and more difficult practice, and there's no reaction either. You might dress one player ahead of another player for a game and there's no reaction – not from the guy going into the lineup or from the guy coming out. I blame it on the fact that, starting at a young age, coaches confront players one-on-one on the bench, in the dressing room, or on the ice, scolding them harshly for mistakes. They rarely do it privately, so in order to cope the players simply don't react. They absorb the comments and show their strength to their teammates by wearing a blank expression. I've seen grown men coaching young ten- or eleven-year-olds go nose-to-nose with a youngster, ranting and raving almost incoherently – and the young player simply takes the medicine and doesn't blink or show any weakness to his playing comrades.

January 16

We got a 2-0 win at Novokuznetsk, in the heart of Siberia, and now our winning streak stands at sixteen games. My media guy tells me that the Super League record was eleven, but that in the days before it was established Red Army might often go a full season with only one or two losses. Still, we're on a nice roll here; let's see how long we can keep it going.

January 17

Winter has come suddenly to Magnitogorsk these last few days. Up until now we've had snow, but the temperatures were pretty moderate. Linda and I haven't experienced a really harsh winter for the last five or six years, so we were thinking, What's it going to be like when it finally comes? For the longest time it was minus five, six, seven; you had to wear your parka and your toque but it was bearable. Then, all of a sudden, it plunged down into the minus-thirty to minus-forty range. I'm a history buff, so right away I started thinking, This is what happened to Napoleon's troops and this is what happened to Hitler's troops. They got caught in just this kind of bitterly cold winter. I've seen guys under their trucks in the morning with blowtorches, heating up the block to loosen up the motor oil to get their cars started. People go outside only when they absolutely, positively have to. When people walk it's with a purpose, to get to where they need to go as quickly as possible. It's been fierce.

I'm still running every day, but it is not a pleasant experience. Usually I just wear one sweatshirt and a nylon jacket and that's it. Sometimes I'll put a scarf around my neck if it gets too cold. But when it gets like this, I'll put on two sweatshirts and wrap the scarf around the front of my face and then tie it at the back of my neck so that it acts as a muffler. By the time I get back to my apartment it's frozen, but it's served the purpose. It filters out the cold air, which is what you really need. The only time the cold really bothers me is when you're running into the cold wind and it's in your face. You can feel spots on your face start to freeze, and that's when you pull the scarf up a little higher. The need to wear a lot of clothing is overrated, I believe. Obviously, there's a lot of really good runner's gear available; I've just never worn much of it. I just wear regular running shoes, regular sweat socks. I'm not into the high-tech gear very much. But you can't enjoy your run because you're just freezing your butt off. Once you get going, after ten or twelve minutes, it's okay, but it's not a lot of fun.

January 18

Our winning streak ended today after we tied St. Petersburg 3-3 at home. Now, instead of winning streak, the media is referring to our "undefeated streak." Simchuk, our number two goalie, started, but he struggled and I had to replace him with Travis Scott. Simchuk doesn't play much for us, so it's important to get him playing, and playing well, before the playoffs. He'll play three games with the Ukraine national team during the Olympic break, so that should help him get sharp again. Just in case anything happens to Travis, we need Simchuk to be ready to go in and be a reliable backup.

January 20

Today the temperature outside is between thirty and thirty-five below. The heating system in our Cherepovets hotel isn't working properly, so the players have taken to wearing their parkas to meals and sleeping in their sweatsuits at night. Reports in the newspaper indicated that there are several deaths every day in Moscow, with street people freezing to death. In many cities, hot water pipes have burst, leaving people to cope with very cold, very damp apartments.

We won 3-1 and played a solid road game. Afterwards, seven players and I took the overnight train to Mytishi, a Moscow suburb, for the All-Star Game.

January 21

The new Mytishi arena opened this past November; it's a beautiful North American-style arena with box suites, a huge replay screen, and a restaurant. Tonight Gennady Velichkin and his wife, Nadia, took us out for dinner along with our translator, Igor, and our Moscow driver, Roman. On the way we passed one massive subdivision after another, filled with huge modern "monster" homes. We could have been in suburban Anywhere, USA.

We loved the restaurant because it reminded us of our cottage back on the lake in Saskatchewan, with its pine siding and its twinkling lights. Inside it was filled with stuffed heads of moose, buffalo, elk, and deer. The menu featured a lot of typical Russian food we'd never tried before. There was a huge appetizer table and everyone sampled something from there. Then we ordered big meals from the menu. They also insisted on ordering black caviar, which of course Russia is famous for. Linda and I, never having developed a taste for the stuff, were looking at each other in dismay as these vast, expensive quantities were delivered to our table. We didn't want to appear rude, so we both tried a little with a spoon and then grabbed big pieces of black bread and smeared them with a little caviar from one plate – and then, when no one was looking, Linda discreetly put them on the floor next to her. The rest she wrapped in some Kleenex and stuffed in a pair of socks she was carrying in her purse. When we got back to the hotel she dumped it down the toilet. We looked at each other, acting like a couple of scheming kids, and had a good laugh over it.

January 22

It's a newer thing, playing an All-Star Game in Russia, but it does have one thing in common with its counterpart in the NHL: there just isn't a lot of intensity. Basically it's a glorified game of shinny, and even though there's not much I can do about that, it just doesn't feel right to me. These players made it here because they're the *crème de la crème*, but what traditionally passes for an All-Star Game rarely has anything to do with the key elements of hockey. I'm coaching the Eastern team with Peter Vorobiev of Lada. Peter speaks very little English and I speak very little Russian. But all through the first period, I'd look down the bench at him and he'd look down the bench at me. Then we'd both look up at the roof. A few minutes later, I'd look down again at him and he'd look at me, and again we'd both look at the roof. We weren't talking, but I'm pretty sure we were communicating our mutual frustration over this state of affairs. At the end of the period I said to my translator: "Ask Peter, right now, what he's thinking about this game." Peter said something about it being "anti-hockey." So I said, "Tell him I agree with that," adding, "I'm not going to be critical, but I'm going to ask the guys to give us a little more hockey."

I had asked Dmitri Yushkevich before the game to act as my translator. So he was right beside me when I said, "Guys, I understand this is the All-Star Game and in three days' time we'll be back working hard and playing regular-season games. But we play games in our league up here" – I held my hand chin high – "and now we're playing down here" – this time, I held my hand close to the floor. "I don't expect you to be up here, but I do expect you to be somewhere in the middle. People want to see some hockey. So all I'm asking is that you skate hard, pass hard, shoot the puck, and keep your shifts short. I don't expect you to block any shots and I'll never ask you to hit anybody because that's not what we're looking for. But this is where we want you to be – here in the middle." Out of the corner of my eye I could see Vorobiev nodding and motioning thumbs-up.

From there, we came out and it was closer to hockey. I'm not sure if the Western team's coaching staff said anything to their players, but because we played differently, they did too – and marginally, it got to look more like a hockey game.

January 23

Back in the Big M on a minus-thirty-seven-degree day, Linda and I dutifully go out and feed the dogs. We'd arranged for Igor's son,

Alexander, to look after them while we were away, but it's something we genuinely enjoy doing. We know it's making a difference in their lives, since when it's this cold they'd spend a lot of their energy just foraging for food. We've become very attached to them, and have even given them names. Our original dog is Lady; another female is Blackie; we call a cute little guy with a bad limp Hopalong or Pegleg; and the last male is Scruffy, which aptly describes his coat.

Our family thinks we've gone over the edge after learning that we've asked one of the arena workers, who's handy with a saw, to construct a doghouse for them. I tried to pay him for his work, but he wouldn't take anything from me, so instead I bought him an ice auger. I know he's a fisherman – a lot of people here fish the river for food and sport – and in winter, when the river's frozen over, you need a heavy-duty auger to saw through the ice. Meanwhile we've put the doghouse in an out-of-the-way place, where we hope no one will steal it.

January 28

I brought home four or five issues of the *Moscow Times*, an English-language newspaper, for Linda. Both of us really miss being able to read a daily newspaper. We have high-speed Internet, and maybe I'm old-fashioned, but for me it can't replace the pleasure of sitting down and reading the newspaper from front to back. Once again, the paper chronicles the staggering amount of corruption that's taking place in Russia. Every day there's a new scandal involving bribery among the country's power brokers, many of whom seem to be willing to sell their influence to the highest bidder. I'm not sure what's more surprising – the fact that this seems to happen on such a monumental scale, or the collective indifference to the latest example of a public official on the take. It's such a fact of Russian life that everyone just seems to accept it.

January 31

At home to Khimik, we managed to get one of our most important victories of the season, a 5-2 win after we trailed 2-1 going into the third period. It wasn't just that we exploded for four goals either. We played with passion, and our physical play was a factor in the result. We didn't rely only on our skill. I'm not sure I could have said that about our team earlier in the season.

Something changed after we acquired Ilya Vorobiev from Lada. You couldn't understand his influence from the stats, because Vorobiev is not a scorer, but his acquisition gave us something that we lacked. He's what you call a greasy player. I had a player like that in Calgary named Ronnie Stern. When you take the puck away from Vorobiev, it isn't as simple as just that. As you skate away, you're going to feel something from this guy. Besides a curse, you're going to feel the lumber coming down. He doesn't respect you. He'll put his glove in your face. This is something we didn't have. We needed more grit. In November, when we had the chance to get Vorobiev, I said, "Take him." He's a shot blocker. He's all the things that we needed. He's changed our team and I'm sure a lot of it has to do with the fact that his dad is a coach.

When you watch his father's team, Lada, in their pre-game skates, you ask yourself, What do they have left? When will this team run out of gas? But they compete. As young as they are, boy, do they play hard. And they're going to make the playoffs with essentially a whole new team since November. There's no question in my mind that Peter Vorobiev is a great coach. Man, is he tough.

He never talks to the guys on the bench. When he goes over to a player, it's never to pat the guy on the back, it's to drill him. So his son plays the way his dad taught him to play – and he's been a terrific contrast and complement to our team.

I've learned a little about Ilya since he came over. His family lives in Spain year-round and he visits them as often as the schedule permits during the season. He's a Russian player but he's on a German passport, so technically he counts as an import for us. I wanted to know how a Russian can be an import in his own country. They tell me that when he went to play in Germany he somehow qualified for a German passport, so he has to play as an import in Russia now that he's home again. He and his wife speak about four languages, including English, so he was easy to integrate into our team. He's a winner, and you've got to have those types of competitive people in your lineup to have any chance come playoff time.

As a coach, one of the exercises I like to go through periodically with my staff is to evaluate our players using a method I call the "circles of influence." What I do is draw a circle to represent the core of our team and then create three or four outer layers of circles around the central core. The inner circle represents the players who have the greatest positive influence on our team. That includes high-profile people like Malkin and other, less-heralded players who may not have the great stats but make a tangible difference in winning and losing. Within each successive outer circle we list players as their influence or importance diminishes. This approach can lead to some interesting discussions, because you need to analyze a lot of factors beyond skill. You consider leadership, game sense, and toughness, factors that often dictate how a player uses his ability in intense, competitive games. In general, my Russian coaching counterparts focus more on skill as opposed to some of the intangibles I value so highly. In a short period of time, Vorobiev has moved right into the critical inner circle because of the way he competes.

There was a time, early on, when I thought we had a lot of fluff on our team. I wondered if we'd be able to get into the trenches against teams that want to play that way. But with Yushkevich, Korolev, Vorobiev, my captain Evgeny Varlamov, and Vladislav Boulin, who played in the Philadelphia Flyers' system for four or five years, I'm not so worried any more. We've got different ways of winning. I think that's why we've been so good – because we can win in different ways. We can win 2-1 and shut the door, but if we get behind, we've got the capability, on a lot of nights, to score those four third-period goals and pull it out, just like we did tonight.

February 1

It seems as if we're on a nine-day shuttle, back and forth to Moscow, every other day. Today, for the third time in nine days, we're on our way back, this time to play Dynamo. What quirky scheduling!

On our way in from the airport I had Igor translate the headlines in the Moscow newspapers. They read "No Pay . . . No Play." Apparently the Dynamo players haven't been paid in over two months – and this is supposedly one of the richest teams in Russia. It sounds as if they have a cash-flow problem and the players finally went public with their demands. They said they wouldn't travel to Novokuznetsk later in the week to play unless they got paid.

Further down, there's also news that Vladimir Plyuschev, the Cherepovets' coach, was fired. He's a good coach, but the team was expected to rank higher than tenth in the Super League standings. According to the newspaper, Cherepovets is planning to hire a foreign coach next year as well. I decided to keep a low profile when the subject of the firing comes up among my assistant coaches. Generally speaking, in most countries, the homegrown coaches can be sensitive about the hiring of foreign coaches.

February 2

At the pre-game skate today I spent a little time talking to Malkin and Kaigorodov after practice, with Igor Korolev handling the translation. I know Igor doesn't like to translate evaluation-type comments to the players, but I needed to get a message across to both players and this is just the most efficient way of doing it. For Kaygo, the message rarely changes. He needs to play with more of an edge. He needs more determination in his game. He wants to play in Ottawa sometime soon, but if he doesn't pick up that part of his game, he'll never last in the NHL. With Malkin, determination isn't an issue. He needs to pass the puck more. He needs to respect the ability of his linemates to play the game. He can accomplish more by passing back and forth with them than simply using them as decoys on every shift.

I'm trying to respect the Russian playing style, but I also want some of these players to understand that in North America – where they both want to play next year – there are subtle, individual things they do to generate more offence. One of the examples I like to use is Gary Roberts, who played for me in Calgary. Gary was always hard to defend against because whenever he was on the wall he'd try to roll and spin and get off the boards first, ahead of the defender, so that he could get to the front of the net first. From there he could establish great screen- and rebound-position so that when someone else shot the puck, he was in a position to tip it, to convert a rebound, or just to celebrate a goal, because the goalie couldn't pick up the shot in time. He also had the ability to protect the puck by using his body to create a wall between himself and the defender. Combining this with quick turnbacks and changes of direction, Roberts would create enough separation to make a pass, or better yet, to go to the front of the net. Korolev, especially, knew and appreciated what a Gary Roberts could do.

In the end, we won the game 3-1 over Dynamo and turned in a solid performance. Kaygo still played too soft, but Malkin had listened.

He played a strong two-way game and made some excellent plays. After the game I talked briefly to Dynamo's head coach Vladimir Krikunov and acknowledged that his team played pretty well, considering they had four good defencemen on the injury list. I also wished him success at the Olympics.

Expectations for a medal are high in Russia and it's going to be a challenge for them. For some reason, while the rest of the hockey world is cracking down on obstruction, hooking, and holding, the Russian Federation decided not to adopt the newly interpreted rules in our league – even though, in theory, Russian hockey is mostly known for its speed, skill, and artistry. That means Krikunov's Olympic team will compete with different refereeing standards from what we're used to in our league. It makes no sense, of course, and is just another example of the Russian Federation marching to the beat of a different (and slightly out of step) drummer.

February 3

Now, here's something completely different: because we've been winning so many games our team is over budget, thanks to the bonus payments that players and staff get after every victory. This may be why we no longer charter when we fly to Moscow – to help keep costs down. The team is tired after another five a.m. return flight. Thankfully, the Olympic break is only a few days away.

February 4

CSKA, the Red Army team, were the visitors tonight, and as always the excitement ran high. When they play here it creates the same buzz that a visit from the Montreal Canadiens does when they go to Calgary or Edmonton. Because of Red Army's long and successful history, it's a game that captivates everyone's attention. Naturally, that helps our players get up for the game as well. We won 2-1, but overall they outplayed us and had the edge in scoring chances. The difference was Travis Scott. He played well in the net and we hung on to win.

When I got back to my office I had a nice surprise waiting for me. Igor Larionov had sent a bottle of wine along with the CSKA people and they'd left it for me. Igor is a real connoisseur and owns interests in wineries all over the world; this wine came from Spain. Along with the wine he'd sent a picture from his playing days in Detroit, which he signed "good luck in Russia, all the best, your friend, Igor Larionov." It was a nice gesture and much appreciated. I don't know Igor all that well, but I was always impressed by his style of play. I remember one time, when I was still coaching the Columbus Blue Jackets, I bumped into him after a practice in Detroit. I was going into the arena and Igor was coming out, and we stopped and talked for a while. He was already forty or forty-one at the time. I asked him, "Igor, when are you going to stop playing?" He answered, "I may never stop." So I said, "You shouldn't. You still play with your head – and your head's still as good as it ever was. That's never going to change. You've always played with your head more than with your legs." He nodded and said, "Yeah, you're right." In my mind, Igor was one of the most intelligent players I've ever coached against. His ability to read his own teammates as well as he read the other team separated him from a lot of players. Some players can read the opposition and react to what they're doing, but they can't read their own teammates. He did both. He was amazing.

After the game we celebrated Nadia Velichkin's fiftieth birthday at a new recreational centre that just opened in town, which offers bowling, billiards, video games, and restaurants. I've learned over the course of the year that the Russians make a big deal out of fiftieth birthdays, so we had a nice night – toasts, lots of laughs – with our new Russian friends.

February 5

Today was supposed to be the start of my one and only week off of the season. Linda and I were scheduled to fly from Magnitogorsk to Moscow to Toronto to Calgary, beginning at eight this morning, but once again, fog delayed our Magnitogorsk flight. As a result, we'd miss all our connections as well. We were really disappointed because we're going back to Calgary to see Andy, Jenn, Sara, and our two grandchildren. We only had seven days and now we only have six. As usual, Linda jumped on the computer and came up with alternative flights to get us to Frankfurt later today. We can overnight in Germany and then fly directly from Frankfurt to Calgary tomorrow.

February 6

After an exhausting travel day, Linda and I are back in Calgary. Meanwhile, our players left Magnitogorsk today – fog permitting – for a nine-day off-ice training session in Dubai. I was originally planning to accompany them, but I haven't been back to Canada since early July, so I approached Velichkin a couple of months ago and asked if I really needed to tag along. Since there were no actual on-ice sessions scheduled, it didn't seem necessary. He agreed, so while we're enjoying a week off with our family, my Russian coaches will oversee a fairly intense mid-season dryland training program. Every morning they'll start with two-and-a-half hours of strength training, plyometrics, and hurdle jumping. Then they'll complete the workout with a forty-minute soccer game. Their afternoons are free, so most of the players took their wives and kids with them to enjoy the sun and heat and relax by the pool. Two other Russian teams also went to Dubai, while still others simply gave their players a week off to holiday wherever they liked. We thought it would be good to give the players a holiday but still keep our fitness level high. By going to Dubai, we've created a win-win situation for both the team and the players.

The only player not in Dubai is Malkin, who made the Russian Olympic team. He'll centre a line of Super League players, playing between Alexander Kharitonov and Maxim Sushinsky, both of whom play for Moscow Dynamo. Because of injuries and withdrawals, there are now seven players from the Russian Super League on the Olympic team. The rest come from the NHL. I'll be interested in watching Malkin compete at this level. I know everyone in our organization is proud of the fact that he's playing for Russia.

February 14

We're back in Magnitogorsk after a much-needed holiday in Calgary, where we visited with family and friends and otherwise revelled in the normalcy of life in Canada – trips to our grandchildren's school, dinners out, a chance for Linda to speak English to everyone she came across. I know it can be hard for her when I'm on the road; sometimes she'll go days without bumping into someone who speaks English. Our players are back from Dubai, and by all accounts they endured the heavy workload with their usual stoicism.

Over seven days they lifted about ten tons of weights, ran twenty-five kilometres to enhance their aerobic capacity, and did three kilometres' worth of sprints.

We're in what amounts to a month-long break from league action, and during the time away our unbelievably successful year – which amazed everyone we talked to – is starting to sink in. Forty-six games into the season, we've lost just three times in regulation. Just three defeats in forty-six games! That's an astonishing winning percentage.

To be honest, I've never had a year quite like this. In some ways I've let it sneak up on me a little. Normally, coaches follow the standings on a daily basis. We have to. Our livelihood depends on wins and losses; lose too many games and ultimately you lose your job. As a coach, you care about how your team did, but you also want to know how everybody else did. Did they close ground? Did they fall back? This year, though, I just wasn't paying as much attention to the other results, even if my Russian colleagues were. Between periods, they'd watch the other games on TV because they worried about the scores. I only ever worried about our own score. I had no idea, for the longest time, how many points ahead we were in first place. If you asked me about our record, most days I couldn't tell you what it was. I only knew that we hadn't lost in a long time. But I never ever got caught up in the success, whereas everybody around me did – to the point where I thought we, as a coaching staff, were maybe getting a little too casual in our approach to some games.

To me, once it's all over, I'll celebrate – if there's a reason to celebrate. My professional record keeps me grounded; I've had good regular seasons in the NHL with the Calgary Flames and not had it translate into playoff success. So I've been around; I have enough experience that I take nothing for granted. But it has been an amazing year. Sometimes I'll call Linda from the road and say, "We won 2-1 tonight," and she'll say, "Again?" because even if you have a great team, you're supposed to lose a game now and then, just as even the weakest teams are supposed to win a game here and there. And we've had reasons to lose. We've had injuries; we lost our number one goalie for three games in November; we've had players away – like Malkin at world junior. We've dealt with fatigue. We went to the Spengler Cup, played five games in six nights, then came back and played eight more league games in the next thirteen nights. There have been all kinds of times when I expected one of those nights with nothing in the legs, nothing in the tank, when we'd get behind by two goals and just wouldn't get them back. But no, it didn't happen. Or at least, it hasn't happened yet.

February 15

Today there was a strange bit of news from Chelyabinsk, one of Russia's most famous hockey cities, the one that produced Sergei Makarov and others for the national team. According to the report, Traktor and Mechel, two teams that play one league below us in the first division, will merge into a single club for the balance of this season. Essentially, Mechel handed over its five best players to Traktor in order to help them win the first division and qualify for Super League play next season. Can you imagine that? One team basically runs up the white flag on its season to help an opponent win it all. The other teams battling to win the first-division title can't be all that happy to see Traktor, Makarov's old team, add five very good players. It'd be like Pittsburgh handing over Sidney Crosby and Marc-Andre Fleury to the Montreal Canadiens to help them make the playoffs.

February 16

Knowing well in advance that we'd have this prolonged break, I had a plan for how we could at least try to maintain the edge we've had all year. My solution is always the same: go right back to the basics. The first three days after the team returned from Dubai, we did an awful lot of one-one, two-two, and three-three work on the checking skills. We reviewed everything: stick on puck, body on body, eyes up. I went right back through our controlled breakout; how we have one man stretch and one man coming from behind so that we have a head-man option and a back-pass option. We go back through it all. We've done it twice already for the earlier breaks in the schedule; this will be the third time. Because coaching is all about repetition and review, I always return to the building blocks. I learned that lesson a long time ago.

In hockey, it eventually all comes down to your ability to play one-on-one. If you play well one-on-one without the puck, you'll have the puck a lot. If you check well, you'll have the puck a lot. If you protect the puck well when you have it, you'll have it a lot. So that's what our training is focused on during this period, and the guys knew it was coming. The pace and the intensity of those drills is hard, hard work, so afterwards we'll taper down, give them a half-day off, and then work our way back up.

We've had a lot of success, and a lot of reasons why we might not have had that success, so I laud the players. We're number one in penalty killing, fourth or fifth in power play, number one in goals-against, number one in goals-for. We lead in so many categories, but I've been around long enough to take nothing for granted.

The other thing that's been good for us is that every time we play we've faced hungry teams. We're a target; for the last two months, teams have come in and said, "Let's beat Magnitogorsk; they haven't lost in two months." They want to be the ones that knock us off. So far, no one's succeeded.

February 17

The Olympics are on television everywhere, and yesterday Malkin played a strong game against Sweden in a one-sided win for Russia. All our players are pumped – at Malkin's performance and that of the team. Meanwhile, Canada lost 2-1 to Switzerland, so I'm keeping a low profile in the dressing room, where the players are watching the games on a big-screen TV.

February 19

It's getting ugly in Turin, with Canada losing again, this time to Finland – and it's no fun for me. I'm taking all kinds of abuse from the players now. The Russians stumbled in the first game against the Slovaks, but they've been good ever since. They could be the team to beat.

February 20

Once we got on a roll this season, we started seeing a lot of teams throw a contain forecheck at us, or a trap as it's commonly called these days, where four or five players skate backwards in the neutral zone, trying to defend against our potent attack. And because the Super League didn't go to a "zero tolerance" policy the way they did in the NHL or in international competition, holdups and/or interference are still common.

The neutral-zone trap is much talked about, but not particularly well understood. Or, more accurately, people have a sense of what a trap does, but not necessarily how to beat it. Strategically, we try to counter the trap by stretching or spreading out their passive 1-2-2 or 1-4 forechecks so that our opponents can't stay compact in the neutral zone, which is what makes a trap so effective. The trap works on the same basic principle as gridlock – there's so much traffic in the neutral zone that often there isn't enough room to make a skilled play. Even if you do, usually someone is permitted to interfere with you, thus slowing the pace of a game down to a crawl. We try to overcome this tactic by having our right wing "stretch skate" behind the opposing defencemen, which pushes them back and creates space between the forwards and defencemen. In some cases the goal is to stretch all five opponents back so that they can't defend the red line. Then we try to carry the puck in.

As a last resort, we'll chip the puck behind the opponents and skate onto it, or if they get there first, try to forecheck hard. Our Russian players like to "stretch" them out, but at the offensive blue line, they'd rather go one-on-one than chip the puck in. This is okay if you have position or a speed advantage, but when the three or four players back on defence are well organized and in position, it can lead to turnovers and often start their counterattack game – which, of course, is what the 1-2-2 or 1-4 system is designed to do in the first place.

Getting the players to buy into our plan took time, and we're getting better every day. Still, I'm constantly amazed at the number of times we'll attack one-against-three when we have virtually no chance of success, and turn the puck over.

Nor do I want us to become a team that relies on dump-ins exclusively, because with our skill level it makes no sense to do so. Nevertheless, there are times when the chip-in is our only option, so we have to do a better job of recognizing those moments.

The challenge, for me, is to get our players to read the defensive alignment in the neutral zone and then make the appropriate decision as they approach the offensive blue line. That's what a tactical practice is all about. You try to create a game situation, and through repetition you hope your players learn to make high-percentage decisions. Because once the game starts, you're behind the bench and they're the ones on the ice making the decisions. As a coach, you can only hope that they make more smart decisions than poor ones. If they understand the logic behind the tactics, they generally make smarter decisions.

February 21

One thing I also believe in is that winning is directly proportional to the number of ice bags your players are wearing after a game. There's no easy way – you have to compete, block shots, and pay the price to win. Our guys are just dead. We've been on the ice since the 15th and we've been putting them through rigorous three-a-day training sessions. Now we're dropping that down to one a day because our schedule resumes in five days' time, on the day of the Olympic final. Then it'll be a sprint to the finish line – five more regular-season games to go and then right into the playoffs.

To get ready for the resumption of play we bused to Ufa yesterday to play an exhibition game. With the freezing temperatures we've had this winter, the pavement on the highway has heaved, so the four-hour bus trip was a non-stop series of natural speed bumps.

Ufa plays tough at home. Given our heavy training loads, I'm not surprised we lost 3-1. It didn't bother me that we lost, either; in fact, it was exactly what I was hoping for. We've been winning so much lately that we're starting to take it for granted. We didn't play our complete lineup – obviously, Malkin is still away at the Olympics – but we had a pretty good lineup, one that should have won that game and didn't. I think the guys remembered that losing is not a great feeling. It got their attention, which was good.

Meanwhile, Blackie, one of our original dogs, is looking rather plump these days and Linda thinks she's going to have pups. Oh, and Linda also adopted a cat. Soon after we came back from Calgary she found a kitten, about seven or eight weeks old, wandering around outside in the snow. It was abandoned, I guess with a lot of others. So we bought cat litter and a cat box, and I don't know how long we'll have him, but he's now our cat. He's the cutest little guy you've ever seen, and he just loves it here.

Also today, Linda took a big hockey bag full of new and used clothes to the orphanage. Our daughter-in-law Sara cleaned out the kids' closets and provided us with lots of quality clothing for the orphans. I know they really appreciated this. If we come back next year, it's something we'll continue to do.

February 22

The news from Turin is disastrous for me, as Canada lost to Russia in the Olympic quarter-finals. I may have to wear a disguise at practice. Naturally, there was a big celebration here. Practice was upbeat; everyone was smiling. I congratulated the players afterwards, but I also warned them that the most difficult game for Russia will be its next one. Big wins often create an emotional vacuum. It will be interesting to see how they rebound two days later against the Finns.

Canada's result, while disappointing, wasn't totally unexpected, given how the tournament went for them. Sometimes it just takes teams longer to blend and for one player to intuitively figure out the other player's game. You can take a lot of good players and put them together and it can click at the drop of a hat. I've been at world championships where you put three guys on a line and think, Well, I'll see how it works out – and you feel like a genius because they develop instant chemistry. Then you put three guys together who you really believe should play well together, and they can't. It looked to me as if Canada never got comfortable in their game. There was no rhythm to it. Rhythm, to me, occurs when you put four or five shifts together in sequence. Do that a couple of times a period and it gives you momentum. That's how you swing a game around. That's how you score your goals. They never seemed to do that. They looked slow. People say the skating game is important, and they're right. But puck movement stimulates the skating game. When the puck starts to move and players feel as if they're going to get it back to make the next play, then your game has a pulse all of a sudden. You really start to feel as if you're in it. Watching Canada play, it didn't look as if they ever had a sense that the next pass was going to be there. It was just two passes and a shoot-in. It just didn't come together. It's too bad.

Right now, everyone here is pumped about Russia's performance at these Olympics. They didn't want to meet Canada so early in the playoff round. Now that they've advanced to the semifinals, there's a feeling that they can really win this thing. Offensively, they've been explosive. And their defence has been much better than people gave them credit for. They may not have the most dynamic defence, other than Sergei Gonchar jumping into the attack, but they play steady in their own end and they get the puck up to the forwards quickly. So their defencemen are the unsung heroes – and Evgeny Nabokov has been lights-out good. He's given them timely goaltending. The only downside from our perspective was that Malkin was suspended for one game after kicking Vincent Lecavalier near the end of the game. I'm wondering if after losing to Canada at the world juniors, there wasn't some residual frustration at work there.

February 23

A word about our playoff system: there are eighteen teams in the league, and only two will miss post-season play. It's come one, come all and follows the old NHL system of the early 1980s, where team number one plays sixteen, number two plays fifteen, and so on. If there's a first-round upset, we'll get the lowest-remaining seeded team that survives because we've clinched home-ice advantage throughout the playoffs. There are teams in ninth or tenth place that could easily upset number seven or number eight in the first round because they're very good. They could beat any team above them – including us. So there could be upsets in the first round and we'd meet the lowest remaining team that advances to the next round. That's our reward for finishing first overall. Also, we have best-of-fives, not best-of-sevens, and that's so dangerous. The first two games are at home; if you split, you could lose in their building, without ever getting back home for a fifth and deciding game. Right now it looks as if the battle for the final playoff spot is between Vityaz, one of the new expansion teams, and Novokuznetsk.

February 24

I did a radio talk show for a Pittsburgh station today and the conversation was all about Malkin. Everyone just assumes he'll go to Pittsburgh next year, but there are two factors no one's talking about. One: Magnitogorsk is building a new arena and Malkin will fill it if he stays here for one year. Two: MMK has a contract with him for the next couple of seasons, and even in Russia, a contract is a contract.

Over in Turin, Russia lost the semifinal game to Finland 4-0 and a mood of depression has descended on our team and on our town.

Like most fans, their loyalty runs deep, and when you lose they can feel betrayed.

February 25

Russia lost 3-0 to the Czechs in the bronze-medal game, and everyone's disappointed that a tournament that started with so much potential ended so badly for them – no medal, nothing to show for what might have been their most promising national team in years.

Linda and I watched the Olympics every night. When you're living abroad, it's hard not to get a lump in your throat watching a Canadian athlete compete on the world stage. One minute you can be so happy for a medal-winning performer and then the next you feel almost heartbroken for someone who may have achieved their personal best but just missed out on the medals. It can hurt just a little more when you come so close. I often look back at our 1988 Olympic hockey team. We finished fourth that year and few people gave us much credit for that result, even though it was still the heyday of the Soviet Union's Big Red Machine. Many of those who dismissed it as a failure had no idea how hard and passionately these athletes competed for Canada. We beat Russia twice in exhibition play leading up to the Olympics, which was probably the worst thing we could have done, since they weren't about to look past us once the Games began. Our own little Canadian Miracle on Ice would have been nice in the hometown Calgary Olympics, but it just wasn't in the cards that year.

Some people may find this odd, but as I'm watching these 2006 Olympics I find I can relate better to the cross-country skiers and speed skaters than to the men's hockey team, given that it's now composed strictly of NHL players. During my nine years with the national program we had a fairly impoverished group, making significant financial sacrifices for the chance to compete in the Olympics. In those days our players received a small stipend – usually between $8,000 and $10,000 – from Sport Canada to defray their living expenses and about the same amount from Hockey Canada. They were officially living below the poverty line for that period of their lives. Our philosophy in those days was simple: we might not be as talented or skilled as our European counterparts, but we would rely on fitness, a strong defensive game plan, and plenty of heart to compete – and it worked for us. In '84, '88, and '92, the Russian Federation didn't allow their players to play in the NHL and the Czechs and Slovaks competed as one nation, so our players faced some of the best talent in the world and didn't give an inch. I was always proud of the fact that our team reflected old-school Olympic values and ideals. So now when I watch the NHL players participate, I'm excited to see best-on-best competition, but I also wonder: with only one or two practices before they play, can they generate any real Olympic spirit? Or, for that matter, can they come together the way any successful hockey team must in order to win? Obviously, the answer this year was a resounding no.

February 26

On the day of the men's Olympic hockey final, we resumed league play with a 4-1 win over Molot. Afterwards we went back to our apartment with two New York Islanders' scouts, Sergei Radchenko and Ryan Jankowski, for pizza and beer and to watch the gold-medal game on TV. They were both here to evaluate Kulemin, who played so well at the world junior championships in Vancouver and is eligible for this summer's NHL entry draft. During the game,

Velichkin phoned on his way back from Turin to inform me that Malkin was emotionally "spent" and shouldn't play in our next game against Lada. Seems like a prudent call to me too.

February 27

Ilya Vorobiev isn't the only ex-Lada player on our roster. In the summer we signed what has become an inseparable defence pair, Alexander Seluyanov and Vladimir Malenkikh. I've taken to calling them the Gold Dust Twins because they're virtually conjoined, on and off the ice. Coming from the Lada School, they're masters of the hack-and-whack style. Even in practice they'll give their own teammates a little extra wood if they try to beat them one on one. Off the ice, they remind me of the Siamese twins in the movie *Stuck on You*. They're polar opposites: Alexander looks like the rock star Jon Bon Jovi; Vladimir like a punch-drunk fighter who's taken one too many hits to the head. They sit together on airplanes, they dress beside each other in the locker room, they share every meal, and they shop and walk together. Even in Magnitogorsk, when Alexander's wife comes to visit, they defy the old expression "Two's company, but three's a crowd" because they spend so much time together. Occasionally I've tried to break them up as a defence pair just to try something new, and invariably it's an unmitigated disaster. They play as one. They know what their partner will do in every situation and it is this chemistry that makes them effective as a pair. Seluyanov's wife is pregnant. If it's a boy, I predict they'll name him Vladimir.

February 28

Today we flew to Samara, then bused one hour to Togliatti to play Lada again. Earlier, at practice, Ilya Vorobiev came up to me and said, "Listen, my dad called, and when we get there he's invited you to come over and have supper with me and my family." So I immediately started wondering what the living is like for him; that he must have something a little better than we have because Peter Vorobiev – who's a substantial guy in hockey – has been in Lada a long time.

Well, when we got there, it was absolutely overwhelming. The kitchen was like something out of a North American design magazine – it was as big as our entire apartment. Then he's got a billiard room, a living room, and a dining room that were all ostentatiously furnished. In his bedroom was a huge aquarium built into the wall. There was a six-person Jacuzzi in his bathroom. I was paralyzed. I couldn't believe it. I thought Velichkin had a nice house – and he does. But this . . . I thought, Where am I? If you had told me it was Rashnikov's apartment, I might have believed it. But Vorobiev . . . oh my gawd! But he's been quite successful over here. He coached the 1998 Olympic team in Nagano. He's finished second with Lada a couple of times. And he was recently named the head coach of Latvia, the host team for the 2006 world championships.

Peter doesn't speak any English, but he speaks a little German. It was awkward because Ilya had to be the translator. His wife also speaks a little German, so we mixed in a little German with a little English and then Ilya translated the rest of the time. Peter's wife, Nina, cooked an unbelievable dinner – pork cutlets, a fish dish, scallops, and shrimps. There were five of us at the table. The dinner could have fed twenty. It was a terrific night and I was really pleased to be invited over. I've coached against Peter many times when I was with the national team and he'd come over to Canada with Russian touring teams. In fact, he brought out a picture at one point and said, "Dave, do you remember? You gave me this picture in 1990." It was a Ken Danby print. We'd had prints framed – of his famous painting of the hockey skates – for all the Russian teams that came over that year. What a nice evening.

March 1

We lost 2-1 in OT against Lada, with the winning goal coming on a four-on-three power play after we had a penalty called against us in overtime. We played poorly overall, spending far too much time in the penalty box. There's also off-ice news: apparently, Kazan's Sergei Zinoviev, the league's fourth-leading scorer, will be allowed to continue playing. Zinoviev had earlier tested positive for a banned substance, but the league's drug commission decided that his abnormally high testosterone levels were natural, and as a result he won't be suspended or penalized in any way.

March 2

The weather in Magnitogorsk is changing; it would appear that spring is on the way. Linda and I did buy the six electric samovars for the orphanage, and she and Igor delivered them today. Julia, the head of the orphanage, wasn't there when the samovars were delivered, but her two assistants couldn't stop thanking Linda and Igor for the gift.

March 4

We won 5-3 against Avangard Omsk, but Travis Scott struggled in goal and I'm starting to get just a little concerned because his chronic hip problems appear to have returned. He had eight or nine days off during the Olympic break when he scooted home to visit family, and since his return he's had a couple of tough outings in a row. It's a quandary you face all the time as a coach. Even though his hip was sore and he wasn't playing well, he wanted to keep going in order to get his game back on track. Understandable. I talked to the therapist, who said his hip isn't going to get worse if he plays. It's just a chronic problem that he's had before and needs to manage. I wanted to keep his spirits up, so I didn't want to tell him I was unhappy with his game. Instead, I asked him if he wanted to take some time off to rest his hip. He said, "No, no." Then he acknowledged, "I've got to be better, so I want to keep playing."

But I'm concerned because he looks slower to me. I can see compensation in his game, some flopping and lying down that I didn't see before. Management is in the midst of negotiating a new contract with his agent for next season, but he's played only about sixty games this season – not the same load as if he'd been in the NHL or in the minors. So hopefully he'll get back to where he was, because this hip problem has definitely slowed him down – and I've noticed just a hint of doubt about his play creeping into our team. To lighten the training load for him, we've decided to bring up our third goalie, Ilya Proskuriakov, from our farm team for the balance of the season.

March 7

We flew Pterodactyl Air to Kazan yesterday and were predictably delayed out of Magnitogorsk because of weather. Today we lost 2-1 to Kazan, marking only our fourth regulation loss of the season and our first since Salavat Yulaev (Ufa) beat us back on November 4. Once again, Scott looked awkward and struggled to get up after making a save.

As for Malkin, he looked tired and was not a factor in the game. He's been back with us for more than a week, but he didn't play against Lada because he just looked dead after returning from the Olympics. He didn't practise for three days, and when we came back from Lada he trained with us for the first time. Then we gave him another day or two off after we played at home against Omsk. I don't know if fatigue's the problem or attitude, because since he's come back it seems as if he's on a mission to do everything by himself again. He played so well in the Olympics that I think he's lost a little respect for the league. Besides fatigue, that was one of my fears – how he'd respond when he came back after playing with the big boys. He's a little bit on his own program right now and we've got to get him out of that quickly.

Afterwards we had a bite to eat, and for the first time in a restaurant over here, there was lettuce in our salads. I asked Igor, our translator, to find out if the restaurant would sell me some to take home to Linda. The restaurant manager sold me four, and Igor and Anders Eriksson bought some as well. She told us that the store across the street sold good fruit, so I was able to buy fresh blueberries, strawberries, and raspberries too.

March 8

More signs of the instability of our league: MVD, the team that plays in Chekhov, had a bit of a revolution because their players hadn't been paid in two months. They were scheduled to play Red Army in their next-to-last regular-season game, but their players went on strike and refused to play. Instead, their farm team played and lost 7-1. It still baffles me, even after nine months, that so many teams in the league are obliged to build new arenas and invest money into their hockey franchises, and yet there's this instability. It isn't just within the fringe teams, either; Lada, which downsized in December, is one of the core teams. Dynamo, the defending champion, is also one of the core teams, and they've gone through another two months without paying their players. They finally got some back pay in January, but then all through February and March they didn't get paid again. In the last week of the season the Dynamo players were very reluctant to go up to Novosibirsk to play. They eventually went, but they weren't sure if they were going to go.

Dynamo is one of the most stable organizations in our league, but when they lost a sponsor in mid-season it created a real cash-flow problem. Yet they still went into the marketplace to bid for players, without having the financial wherewithal to pay the ones they already had. They signed Vaclav Pletka, who was a pretty good player in the Czech league; he stayed five or six days and then left. Pavel Rosa, who's played for them the last couple of years, left in December because he had three or four months' worth of salary owing – and even some money from last year that still hadn't been paid. So I don't understand how they go out and sign all these players without having the budget. They just do it – and damn the consequences.

March 9

Linda and I went for a walk after practice because we haven't seen one of our dogs, Blackie, for about a week. Up until now, she hasn't missed a single meal. She often sleeps in a doghouse inside a warehouse yard, and so we looked there. To my surprise but not to Linda's, there was Blackie with six puppies. In a manner of speaking, we are proud parents again.

March 10

The Fish is giving us problems again. He can't play tonight because he's still recovering from another one of his mysterious injuries. As per usual, we kept him on the ice for extra work after our pre-game skate along with the other players who weren't dressing. Fedor Kanareykin smelled alcohol on his breath. This is the third or fourth time he's had an episode; usually it happens after a break in the schedule, when he finds himself at loose ends and ends up going on a bender. We've warned him time and again, and ultimately put him on a zero-tolerance policy. He knew that if he showed up one more time after going on a bender, he'd be in trouble. So after practice we held a meeting and told him to pack his bag for our farm team. He can practise with them until he proves to us he deserves another chance to play.

In our final game of the regulation season we played Yaroslav Lokomotiv, with nothing at stake but pride and the desire to enter the playoffs on a high. They, meanwhile, needed a win to finish in second place. We played our best game since the Olympic break ended, won 4-1, and put out a really good effort. I noticed that their coach, Yurzinov, patiently stood behind the players for the first two periods, but that by the third period he'd had it. He got in front of them, often ignoring the play on the ice so that he could give his players an earful. It didn't help. They finished third.

Novokuznetsk grabbed the final playoff spot, while Vityaz and Molot missed out. I felt sorry for Vityaz because they came so close as an expansion team. Their top player was the ex-San Jose Shark, Korolyuk, who played at the Olympic Games. In the fourth game of the Olympics, Korolyuk got injured and never played another game. They had five games left to catch either MVD or Novokuznetsk and couldn't do it because their best player was sidelined.

Dave and Evgeny Malkin after practice. Malkin left for the Pittsburgh Penguins of the NHL after Dave's year in Russia.

PART 4 **SPRING**

March 10

I SPENT THE WHOLE YEAR TRYING NOT to look at the Super League standings, but now that they're final, I can't help thinking about what an extraordinary regular season it's been, even with a couple of our post-Olympic hiccups. We finished first overall with 127 points. On the last day of the season, Ak Bars Kazan held off Lokomotiv Yaroslav for second place. Kazan finished with ninety-eight points, twenty-nine behind us. We won thirty-eight games in regulation and four more in overtime. We also tied four, lost once in overtime, and lost four other games in regulation. Think about that for a moment: only four regulation losses in fifty-one regular-season games. It's an extraordinary accomplishment; it shattered the Super League record. We scored 175 goals, the most in the league. We gave up seventy-five goals, the fewest in the league. We play the sixteenth-placed team, Novokuznetsk, in the opening round of the playoffs. From here on in it's a series of best-of-five playoff rounds. As the top seed, as long as we continue to advance, we play the lowest-remaining seed in the competition. It means that if there's an upset in the first round we benefit by virtue of finishing first overall.

Playoffs are to a hockey team what Christmas is to kids – something they look forward to all season. Now that they're upon us, I sense a new level of excitement in our dressing room. During our pre-playoff meeting with the players, both Velichkin and our assistant GM, Oleg Kuprianov, addressed the team. They talked about discipline on and off the ice and the importance of the playoffs to the organization. When it was my turn to speak, I told the players that we may not be the best team on paper, but we're the most consistent of the best teams.

There's been a running joke in our dressing room this year about the influence of Viktor Gudzik, our pharmacologically inspired fitness coach. Gudzik can be a boastful man, and all season he's been telling everyone that the key to our success has been his recovery program. So today, after I finished speaking, Velichkin stood up and did a strange thing. He shouted, "Gudzik is magic! Pharmacology is important in today's athletics. Every team in the Super League wants Gudzik – he is magic!" When he left the room everyone was howling with laughter, which I think – I hope – is what he intended. I know for a fact that the players are miffed that Gudzik gets or takes so much credit. Our success is based mostly on their character and determination, and not on any unique fitness or recovery program.

Back in July, in my first few weeks with the team, I wasn't sure what I had. Now I'm confident that I can go to war with this group. We still have some fluff, players who are unwilling to pay the price to win, but we have enough of the other kind – the heart-and-soul guys – to make me feel good about our chances. One thing I can safely say: there is a night-and-day difference between these players and the ones I had last year, back when I was coaching in Germany.

It was right around this time a year ago that I reached one of the lowest points of my career; I got fired in Hamburg, Germany, with just weeks to go in the regular season. We'd gone through a season of unbelievable injury to key players. We were down to five or six imports out of the eleven we were permitted in our lineup, and had to borrow five players from Pierre Page's Berlin Eisbaren farm team to complete the season. Still, we were battling and about to sneak into the playoffs – just barely – when they came in and told me, "We want to make a change, you're too hard on these guys."

I packed up my stuff and drove home, thinking, Holy mackerel! It doesn't matter who you are, or what profession you're in, getting fired shakes your confidence. As I looked back on that time, it became evident that I was miscast coaching in Germany. I had an expectation level for training and competing that they didn't come close to matching. At the time, I wondered if it was just me; that my expectations were too high and that as I got older I was getting too far removed from a new professional hockey reality that I couldn't relate to any more. And when I first met this team in Magnitogorsk, I asked myself the same questions. I thought, It could be good, but it could crash real early too – because I might not fit. In Germany I was always compromising, all the time. I couldn't understand why these guys wouldn't lift weights after practice. It confused me, until I finally figured it out. They were on a European vacation. They'd had it with coaches who wanted to push them – that's why they came to Europe in the first place. I couldn't grasp that at the time and I still have problems with that sort of attitude. To me, no matter what stage you're at in your career, you never stop pushing yourself to be your best. I don't think there's anything wrong with that. I don't think I need to apologize for believing that either.

So this has just been a much better fit for me and for the way I approach coaching. Maybe I should have come here earlier in my career because the Russian stoicism in training and preparation matches my personal philosophy. I don't know if we necessarily outwork any teams, but we do work as hard as everybody else does. Preparation is my job; it's up to me to make sure that no situation develops in the game that we're not prepared for.

Every evening after supper, as Linda worked at her computer, I'd sit at my desk and work on my practice plan for the next day. She'd sometimes say, "Why don't you just repeat a good practice you've done in the past? Why do you have to spend so much time planning tomorrow's practice?" I'd always give her the same answer:

"Tomorrow is a different moment in time and our needs are different. This is not about opening up another can of soup. This is about being creative in the kitchen." I spend a lot of time getting organized because I want us to practise efficiently. I don't want to waste a lot of valuable energy accomplishing very little. As a coach, you can't confuse activity with productivity. There's an expression we use – work hard but work smart – because once the season begins, managing fatigue is one of your biggest challenges. You want to practise to stay sharp, but never to the point where you're responsible for sending a tired team onto the ice. The sheer number of games, the travel, and the intensity of the competition will all fatigue your team enough as it is. The coach doesn't need to add anything to it.

My Russian players seemed satisfied once the season was in full swing because we practised hard, but not long. We kept the pace high. We tried for variety. The focus of our practice was usually related to one of two things: the video review of our last game or a look ahead to the next opponent on our schedule. That's especially important now, in the playoffs, when we're playing a best-of-five series as opposed to just a single game. After practice we'd keep our young players and taxi-squad guys on the ice for extra work, but it amazed me to see Korolev, Yushkevich, and now Anders Eriksson stay out after every practice as well, working on little things to improve their games.

Their professionalism really permeated our team. Now after almost every practice only a handful of players leave the ice right away. This kind of individual work after practice can make a real difference in the outcome of a game, and these Russian players, unlike my guys in Germany, don't seem bothered by it at all.

March 11

One of the first questions I was asked when I came to Russia was, "Would I coach like a Russian?" That puzzled me, so I asked in turn: "How does a Russian coach?" The answer was "The unit approach," meaning players grouped in five-man units, which is the tradition in Russian hockey circles. In the days of the KLM line, the same three forwards – Krutov, Larionov, and Makarov – would always go on the ice with the same two defencemen, Fetisov and Kasatonov. That never, or rarely, varied. So my answer was, "No, we're not going to coach that way here." I like to mix and match. For example, I sometimes play my third unit on the power play because they're quite good at it, but I'll use my top two defencemen with that third forward line. I do all the things the North American coaches do that no one else here does. Even Kazan's Zinetula Bilyeletdinov, who coached extensively in the NHL, has gone back to the Russian approach.

There was a time when the players questioned why we did it this way; even my assistant coaches wonder about it sometimes. Fedor Kanareykin changes the defencemen, but it's not easy for him because he wants to match up, first block against first block, and so on. I keep telling him, "Don't worry about keeping the units together. Just get me two defencemen on the ice." If I quickly turn and send out a different line, he wants to scramble and try to come up with the defence pair that normally goes out with that line. I tell him not to bother. I say to him, "Just go with the same two defencemen you were going with before. . . . As long as we've got five guys out there, I'm happy. If someone criticizes us afterwards, it'll be on my head."

Of course, what I'm trying to do is to get matchups, which no one else seems to think is important here. There are times when I can get Malkin, the number one player in the league, out against a team's fourth line – and even our guys don't realize what I'm doing. Malkin himself sometimes doesn't understand. Once, just before the Olympic break, in a game against Red Army, he turned back and looked at me as if to say, "Why are we not going out? It's our turn." And I said, "I'll coach, you play." See, I was putting my checking line out against their top centre, Sergei Mosiakin. Mosiakin is right there with Malkin in the scoring race – and Malkin desperately wants to win the scoring title. What he didn't understand is, if I'm checking Mosiakin, Mosiakin isn't going to get anything tonight and we're going to win the game, so anything Malkin gets, scoring-wise, is gravy for him. Sometimes I'll change my rotation to get my first line out against their fourth line, and I just know they're going to score – but our guys don't get it. It's sweet, really sweet.

Sitting out the game last week in Lada didn't help Malkin's bid for the scoring title, and today he got even more bad news. Because of the perception that points are awarded differently depending on who's refereeing and where the game is played, the Super League decided to review on video the points given to all the top scorers in the league. As a result, Malkin lost four assists and dropped to second in the scoring race behind Mosiakin. I'm also told that the scoring race will continue on into the playoffs. In North America and in other European countries that race includes only regular-season games, whereas in Russia, if the top scorer in the regular season played on a non-playoff team, he'll have no chance to win the scoring title because his season is over already. Someone like Korolyuk, who played in Vityaz, is going to sink like a stone once the playoffs get underway, because he didn't qualify.

March 12

A player committee of Varlamov, Korolev, Yushkevich, Atyushov, and Boulin came to see me today about The Fish's problems. They were nice about it. It wasn't as if they were contesting what I was doing. But they said, "Look, we know him, we know he's got this problem, we know what you're doing and why you're doing it, but he's been with this team for a couple of years and he's just going to get worse if you do this." I said, "I appreciate that you care enough about him to come to me like this; what do you propose that we do?" So they said, "We know he shouldn't play, but can he come back to the dressing room and work out – and prove to you that he should be given a chance to play?" I said, "Yup, okay, I don't know if it'll work out, but let's do that."

I agreed to allow him back mainly because I was impressed that his teammates wanted to help him get his life back on track. The Fish, meanwhile, agreed to attend a treatment centre and to enter a rehabilitation program. So we've got him back now and we'll see where it goes from here. There are enormous problems with alcoholism in Russia. He's a fine talent, born in '83, with skill coming out of his ears. He's been drafted and the NHL team that owns his rights is always phoning about him, but he can't play in the NHL until he gets this problem under control.

March 13

For a first-round playoff opponent we drew Metallurg Novokuznetsk, a team from the heart of Siberia, and the series began tonight. Before the game I walked into the dressing room for a cup of coffee and saw someone standing there whom I'd never seen before. I asked some of the players and they didn't know who he was either. Neither did Fedor, my assistant. Finally I found out the answer: he's our new massage therapist. We've got three now. It turns out he's the son-in-law of one of our other coaches. I'm sure he's a nice guy and a good massage therapist, but it's our dressing room and we were never consulted. I just shook my head.

I need to talk to Velichkin. Both he and Kuprianov have been around a lot more in the last couple of weeks, just hovering everywhere. The last game of the season they came on the road with us to Kazan, which they don't do very much. I could tell they were both getting really nervous about the playoffs. Apparently, at this time of year, your managers and assistant managers all get very active and as an unhappy byproduct, tend to get in your way. So we're in Kazan and I go into the room to talk to our players before the game and there's Velichkin right there. He's there for my pregame talk, he's there between periods, and he's on the bench for our game. The next day we come back, and he's in my office. He's never in my office. I'm thinking, What the heck is going on here? Maybe I'm superstitious, but we've had such a good regular season that I don't want to change anything now that the playoffs are here.

Tonight we started the game really well with a 3-0 first-period lead. Kulemin opened the scoring for us and then Malkin scored twice, on assists from Yushkevich. We ended getting a late goal from Platonov in the third period to win 4-0, with Travis Scott getting the shutout and a third-star selection.

Even so, I'm not completely thrilled. Once we got ahead early, we thought it was going to be easy and stopped playing hard. Our third period was especially awful, as we took a lot of penalties and created lots of counterattack opportunities for Novokuznetsk by turning the puck over in the neutral zone.

March 14

Tonight we played one of the most dramatic playoff games I've ever been involved in. As a team, we were better than we were in the opener, but we were behind by a goal with about ninety seconds to go when I pulled Travis Scott for the extra man, trying to get a tie.

With six seconds to go, Stanislav Chistov – our young, talented, maddeningly inconsistent forward who briefly played for the Mighty Ducks the year they went to the Stanley Cup final – scored an incredible goal to tie the game 2-2. In the Russian league, if a game is tied in regulation, we play ten minutes of sudden-death overtime and it's four-on-four, not five-on-five, all the way. If the game is still tied, then it goes to a shootout.

Now, I need to preface this by saying that after our first game of the series I was deeply upset with Chistov, who has a tendency to do that to his coaches. After we went up 3-0, both he and Malkin, who were playing on the same line, started doing their own thing instead of concentrating on team goals. So today at practice I told Chistov that I was not really thrilled with the way he'd been playing lately. He was turning the puck over too much. He was trying to beat everybody one-on-one. In short, he wasn't good in the first game and, for the first fifty-nine minutes of the second game, he wasn't good again. Tonight, for example, on our first goal, he had the puck right in the slot with the goalie down and what did he do? Shoot? No, he passed the puck off to the side to Nurtdinov, who had no shooting angle at all from where he stood. But Nurtdinov, bless him, has a laser shot; he wired it and scored from an unbelievable angle, so Chistov got an assist anyway, even though he made the wrong play and deserved nothing. So I moved him from the first line to the third line with Korolev and Vorobiev, where Chistov can turn it over all night and those two guys will always cover up for him. But now we're a goal behind and down to the last two minutes of the third period, so I called a time out and – don't ask me why – put Chistov out there again.

For a minute and a half we controlled the puck and did a lot of good things, but they cleared it out with about sixteen seconds to go and it looked as if we were done. But Yushkevich gathered up the puck for one last rush, and I looked up at the clock and there were fourteen seconds to go. Yushkevich made a quick pass to

Kaigorodov, who got to the line and popped it across to Platonov. Platonov beat a guy and slid it across to Chistov, who was wide open, one-on-one with the goalie. This is it! I thought. But no, Stan tried to deke the goalie, lost control of the puck, and was now falling down behind the icing line. But unbelievably, on the way down, he swept the puck to the front of the net. This last-gasp centring pass hit the goalie on the back of the leg and went in. That was the tying goal that forced overtime. There were six seconds left on the clock – and we went on to win the game in a shootout.

That, in a nutshell, sums up Stanislav Chistov. He can drive you crazy one moment and in the next you want to give him a big hug. When Mike Babcock was still coaching Anaheim, just before he signed with Detroit, I called him up as a courtesy to tell him that Chistov would probably sign with us and skip out on the NHL. So we started talking about him and Mike's exact quote to me was, "We don't think he wants to score, we think he wants to be cute." I've kept that quote in mind all year and he was exactly right. Chistov has amazing skill. You just have to accept that he'll do some things that'll make your hair stand up – but then he'll also do some things that make you stand up.

The one thing that experience has taught me is that a playoff series can turn on the smallest of developments. If that tying goal doesn't go in and the series is tied 1-1 and now we need to go into their building for two games, who knows what could happen? There are eight thousand people in that rink when it's sold out and it's not an easy place to play. One little event can change everything. Once, when I was coaching the Flames, we were in the seventh game of a playoff series against the San Jose Sharks and twice in the third period we hit the knob of Wade Flaherty's goalie stick. The puck stayed out and we lost the series in double overtime. That's how it can sometimes go in sport. On both the goals we scored in regulation, Chistov did exactly the wrong thing – he passed the puck from a scoring area to a non-scoring area . . . and we scored anyway.

Those are plays that probably shouldn't have worked out, but they did. It's an amazing game sometimes.

March 15

It's springtime in Magnitogorsk now; the temperature is above zero and everything's melting, but today we travelled three hours into Siberia – for Game 3 against Novokuznetsk – and found not a hint of spring. When we got off that plane it was minus sixteen, even colder with the wind chill, and snow was falling. It felt as if we'd taken a detour right back into the depths of winter. Magnitogorsk is on the fringes of Siberia, but Novokuznetsk is right in its heart. If you go to a map and find Mongolia, from its very western edge just go directly north up to the middle of Siberia – that's where you'll find Novokuznetsk. It's the farthest point east of any team in the league. It's a steel city and its nickname is also Metallurg, same as us, because they too are sponsored by a steel company. Before the game we were told that the Novokuznetsk management guaranteed every player US$7,000 if they won, so we knew their motivation would be high.

March 16

We had three players – Yushkevich, Vorobiev, and Malenkikh – hurt in the shootout win in Game 2; all of them injured blocking shots. Two of them got hurt in one sequence because Chistov and Malkin left the zone too early and didn't get the puck out. Yushkevich needed to go down to block a shot and it came back to the point, so this time Vorobiev dropped down and blocked the shot. Then, as he rolled over, because he was in pain, Vorobiev blocked a second shot with his back, and now it's so sore he can hardly skate. We're not sure if he can play or if he can take faceoffs, but he tells us there's no way he's coming out.

This guy has an unbelievable heart – and pain threshold. On the first Novokuznetsk goal, Vorobiev loses the draw, it goes back to the point, and the guy back there just lasers it into the net. I'm thinking, Poor Ilya, because he usually wins faceoff after faceoff for us. So he comes to the bench and he looks as if he's died, he's so upset. But the next time we need to win a faceoff, I put him back out and do you know what? He didn't lose another faceoff for the rest of the game. Not one – and we won 3-2 to sweep the best-of-five series three straight.

Typical of the way things can go in the playoffs, the winning goal is scored by Boikov, his first of the year. It wasn't much of a goal, but they all count, right? We won the faceoff in their zone. The puck came back to him at the point. He was being pressured, so he just took a wrist shot that skipped once and went right through the goalie's legs. It was unbelievable, and not just because it was the first game he'd played in the series. I knew, from two visits here during the regular season, that it's a hard rink to play in because it's so noisy, so I proposed taking out Biryukov, our young defenceman who played at the world juniors, and putting in Boikov because he's got more experience. Everybody agreed that was a good idea, and then he goes on to score the winning goal.

But that's how playoff series are won – by unlikely scoring heroes and because players such as Ilya Vorobiev pay the price on every shift. He just competes, and the guys who compete pay a physical price. The guys who float and get the headlines haven't got a scratch. He's changed our team for the better in so many ways. We're playing with more grit. I reward Ilya with more ice time for the way he plays, and other guys see that and they think, If that's how you do it, I guess I better do it too.

March 17

The post-game press conferences here aren't much different from what I'm used to. Unless you're trying to send a message through the newspapers about something, they amount to much ado about nothing. Today, though, I learned something from the Novokuznetsk coach about what happens once a team is eliminated from the playoffs. In North America, it just means you're on the golf course a little sooner. Not here. Their coach was asked, "What's next?" He answered, "Well, we have five days off. Then we go back on the ice for three weeks of two-a-days." Then they get two weeks off and come back for three more weeks of training before they finally get their summer break.

If we get knocked out in the next series, I'll go home, but the team will stick around and train. They never give these guys four months off. They'll be on the ice until the end of April. They'll do dryland training for a couple of weeks in May. Then they get their six- to eight-week summer break. And when they shut it down, they really shut it down. You may give them an off-season conditioning program, but it goes in the bottom drawer somewhere. They just collapse and do nothing.

There was one upset in the first round so far, with Lada knocking off Moscow Dynamo, the defending champions, in four games. In addition, the eleventh-place team, Neftekhimik, is going to a fifth game against sixth-place Mitishi Khimik. If Neftekhimik wins, they're our next opponent; if not, we'll face Lada, Peter Vorobiev's team. And Ilya Vorobiev will get to play against his old teammates.

March 18

The one thing I don't like in this series – something that's been bothering me for a couple of weeks now – is the way Velichkin continues to hover around, getting in the way, spooking everybody with his presence. The other night, playing against Novokuznetsk in the game we won in the shootout, I went into my office after regulation and before the overtime period began, and I could see that he was just coming apart. I'm trying to coach. I'm telling the guys, "Let's try to win the period," but we're also reviewing our shootout list, in case we get to that, and who we should put in and what the order should be. So Velichkin listens to all that and then, when we come out, he's not on the bench exactly, but he's at the end of the bench, standing there, watching. When we won the shootout, he went goofy. Then we moved on to Novokuznetsk for Game 3 and he was at the video meeting and in the dressing room. They have a very small coaching room there for a very large staff. But Kuprianov comes in and Velichkin comes in and they get their computers out and they've got their cellphones going. They're taking calls and chit-chatting and having coffee and I'm sitting there thinking, I've got to get ready for the game. So finally, I left – but I also said to my assistant, Fedor, "We've got to talk to them, because they can't do this. It's too much of a distraction."

Before the game, I told the players a little story: "Guys, we're up 2-0 and it's going to be a difficult game tonight. However, if we have to come back and play Game 4 here tomorrow night, it's going to be even more difficult. But we've got the knife to their throats. Now it's time to cut their throats and watch them bleed."

Oh, was Velichkin ever pumped. He just loved that. I don't think he or Kuprianov are cut out for the pressure. I asked Fedor, "Is this common?" He said, "Yes, that's the way it is in Russia. They think it's a show of support." They may think that, but I don't see it that way at all.

March 19

Linda and I have decided to take our adopted kitten, Rocky, back to Canada, so we bought a carrying case today and arranged for his rabies vaccination with a veterinarian. Rocky is going to live in Saskatchewan with our daughter Jenn, who loves cats and has a young kitten, Charlotte, who will be good company for Rocky.

Today, Khimik beat Neftekhimik in the final game of the opening round, so we'll be playing Lada in the quarter-finals against their all-teen lineup and with my new friend, Peter Vorobiev, behind the bench. It should be interesting.

March 20

Ah, progress. We discovered a brand-new restaurant the other day called the Dublin Irish Pub, and their burgers are great. We've dined there two out of the last three days. Sometimes, when you discover something new that reminds you of home, you can go a little overboard at first. You find these faux Irish pubs all over Europe now, and they can surprise you with their authenticity – imported beer, pub food, and in this case beautiful stained-glass windows. Magnitogorsk – for better or worse – is gingerly putting one foot forward into the twenty-first century, even if that means importing someone else's culture. Then something else happens that makes you realize that the past – Russia's Wild West days – is still lurking not too far behind.

Dennis Abdulin, who's playing for Lada, had a family tragedy occur earlier today. Abdulin is a young player from Magnitogorsk who couldn't crack our lineup at the start of the season, so we loaned him to a second-division team in Chelyabinsk. Then Lada liked him and picked him up after their downsizing back in

November. Anyway, Abdulin's brother lives in Chelyabinsk and he gets himself involved in a love triangle. He's got a girlfriend who a militia guy thought was his girlfriend too. Apparently, three members of the Russian militia decided to make a big deal about that. They chased Abdulin's brother, by car, from Chelyabinsk. The brother got to within sixty miles of Magnitogorsk, on the highway, when they finally caught him and all shot him down, execution-style. Yikes, just when you think there's some normalcy to life, something like this happens.

March 21

I'm worried about Travis Scott's hip. He played so well for us before the Olympic break – we didn't lose a home game with him in goal all season – but like a lot of goalies nowadays, he has chronic hip soreness and it has gotten worse lately, so we've taken him to an acupuncturist. The muscles around his hips are so tight; our hope is that this will alleviate some of his problems.

March 22

Ever hear of Murphy's Law – that if something can go wrong, it will? The first game of the Lada series was a Murphy's Law kind of game. We lost 2-1, marking the first time we've lost at home all season; it was also Travis Scott's first-ever Super League loss in regulation. On the second shift, Pestunov, my young twenty-year-old centre, tore the ligaments in his shoulder and he was out. At about the nine-minute mark of the second period, Malkin drove wide to the net, shot, and just as the goalie covered up the rebound, poked at the puck again. Abdulin (the murdered man's brother) saw Malkin poking at the puck and was so pent-up with emotion that he just attacked him. He was swinging like a crazy fool. Malkin backed off a few steps but eventually had no choice but to swing back – and they both got tossed out. Think about this: Malkin gets tossed out for fighting Abdulin, a player whose rights belong to us. But his brother has been executed by these militia guys two days before and he missed practice yesterday because he's with his family, mourning his loss. Three policemen from Chelyabinsk have been arrested now and charged with the murder of Abdulin's brother. Abdulin, a fourth line guy for them, took our number one centre out of the game – and we lost 2-1. Not a very good tradeoff for us. And since Abdulin's from Magnitogorsk, he and Malkin have obviously played together; they've known each other since they were boys. Before the game I felt so sorry for the kid, but by the middle of the game I was mad at him myself. I can safely say that in more than thirty years of coaching, I've never seen anything quite like this happen before – that a grief-crazed brother attacks our best player and gets him tossed out and we can't come back in the game. That's the thing about being in Russia. You think you've seen it all, and then you get over here and realize you ain't seen nothing yet.

March 23

We rebounded in a big way today, with a convincing 7-0 win in which Dmitri Yushkevich scored three goals, a Super League playoff scoring record for a defenceman. It really was a statement game for our team. We couldn't afford to lose, but we also needed to prove something to ourselves. Tonight our best guys were our best guys. Yushkevich was spectacular and his defence partner, Anders Eriksson, was excellent too. Before the game I said to our guys,

"Look, it's very simple. We've had a terrific season, we've been the most consistent team in the league, so just believe in yourself. Don't let this unsettle you. You know how to play. You know how to compete. If we can just stay collective, we'll be fine. We've just got to keep the puck in motion. If we do, we'll spread them out and we'll get our game going." I'm not a prophet or anything, but we really moved the puck well and we were awesome on the power play; we just pummelled them.

But we didn't get away completely unscathed. Long after the game was decided, one of our guys speared one of their players in front of their net. Just as he went down, Varlamov, our captain, took a shot from the point that accidentally hit the Lada player. So Varlamov skated over to apologize and the guy gets up and cold-cocks Varlamov with a punch. Down goes Varlamov in a heap. He's knocked unconscious and they carried him out on a stretcher.

Velichkin, our manager, went crazy. He told the media that Varlamov was in a coma, had broken vertebrae, and that it was one of the worst incidents he had ever witnessed. He then instructed his secretary to write a letter to the league; both he and Rashnikov, our owner, signed the complaint. Although Varlamov definitely suffered a concussion, it wasn't as serious as Velichkin made it out to be. He'll be lost for the rest of this series and possibly a couple of games if we make it to the semifinals, but the doctors tell me he should be able to play again later in the playoffs.

With Varlamov out, it's going to mean more ice time for Yushkevich and Eriksson. Ever since Eriksson signed with us after Christmas, I've paired him with Yushkevich. Both played extensively in the NHL, both speak English fluently, and they've been a nice fit on the ice. Eriksson, a Swede who won a Stanley Cup for Detroit, has been a good fit off the ice as well. He's proven to be quite a character. The more I worked with him, the more I realized how popular he'd become within our team in such a short period of time. At pre-game meals he'll deliberately go sit at a table with five

Russian guys who speak no English. Often, Seluyanov will be one of them. Seluyanov may be the grumpiest guy you've ever met; he's always sour about something. Anders, by contrast, usually has a smile on his face and he's always talking. He talks incessantly. So he'll sit there with these five Russians and he'll carry on both ends of the conversation. He'll ask them about their sticks, or if they want sauce on their steak, or ketchup for their potatoes. He'll say, "Nice day today, weather's great, my family's fine, thanks, Sely, for asking." He'll go on and on. I'm a great believer that humour's the lubricant that helps teams create chemistry. Those antics in the dressing room, that's how you build a team – or they help, anyway.

March 25

We played an excellent, tough playoff game and won 4-3 to go ahead in the series 2-1, but we were in the penalty box the whole night. Lada was doing so much acting on the ice to draw penalties that our team was getting frustrated by their antics. So on my way to the post-game press conference, I decided to address the issue with the media. All the big Moscow newspapers were there, so I just teed off. I went on and on about how ridiculous the theatrics were in this series. I said, "I don't fault the refereeing because there's so much of this going on that it's hard to tell if a guy's been highsticked or clipped with a stick or an elbow or what." I added, "It's a man's game, not a boy's game. It's a man's league we're playing in." Then I talked about sportsmanship and how in North America we were often criticized for allowing players to fight. Here fighting was viewed as unsportsmanlike. I suggested that acting was an even greater sin because it took no courage, whereas it took a lot of courage to drop your gloves, fight, and possibly lose in front of thousands of fans. I concluded by saying, "If the Russian Super League wants to solve the problem of diving, they should make fighting only a major penalty, and not a game misconduct as well, because then some of these actors would have to be accountable for their actions."

Penalties almost killed us a couple of times tonight. We were up 3-2 with about eight minutes to go and playing four-on-four when Chistov took the stupidest penalty he could possibly take in the offensive zone to give them a four-on-three power play, which they proceeded to score on to tie the game 3-3.

Was I ever mad at him! Still, with Chistov, you always hope for redemption. It came with about three-and-a-half minutes left when we finally went on the power play. About halfway through, we hadn't scored, so I called a timeout because I didn't want to switch to my second unit. I wanted my first unit on the ice, but I changed it up. I put Malkin out with Chistov and Kaigorodov, and what happened? Chistov scored the goal that won the game. That's him. You couldn't get a better goal. In the course of one game, you can be so impressed in one moment and in the next, you wonder what's he doing.

Psychologically, the pivotal moment in the game came during the second period with the score tied. Once again, we were killing what seemed to be an endless supply of penalties when Igor Korolev went down to block a shot. There was a collision, the other guy fell too, and Igor received a skate cut for twenty-three stitches. It was so bad that our doctor was practically throwing up. He told us, "Igor's out for the game for sure." I thought, Well, we'll see. So they took him to the dressing room, where Igor got mad at the doctor because he was taking all day to get the job done. He thought Igor was done for the night. Igor, meanwhile, barked, "Get me sewed up, I'm going back." The doctor said, "You can't go back." Igor said, "Get the stitches in because I *am* going back." So the doctor finally got off his butt, put the stitches in, and about three minutes into the third period, down the runway, here comes Igor Korolev with a great big patch over his eye, blood all over his sweater and his face. He was back. Over here, it's common for a guy to have a temperature of one or two degrees above normal and not play. They have this theory that you could develop heart problems if you play with a fever. I've never heard of that theory, but they have it here. So when Korolev came back and played just great, it made such a difference to our morale.

He's playing like crazy and so is Yushkevich, who has five or six goals. All my veteran guys, who everybody over here thought were too old, are carrying the ball. Velichkin never acknowledged that I was right about insisting we get these two guys, but just before the playoffs started he had a conversation with Mark Gandler, the agent for these players, and told him that we wanted to sign both for next year. I think they understand that in the end, you win with these types of warriors. You need skill, but you have to have guys that glue everything together.

March 26

We clinched the series in four games with another close 2-1 win. Lada gave us a scare; they played like hell. They were just possessed. They work, work, work. They made mistakes and covered them up with a great effort. It was a hard series – high-paced, by far the fastest pace of any of the playoff series I've seen on tape. I give them a lot of credit; they played very well.

After my refereeing diatribe made all the newspapers, I got the result we wanted. The referee called a wonderful game. They were diving; he'd just give them the dive sign. He got fooled a couple of times, but mostly he did a very good job. And I'm guessing their coach, Peter Vorobiev, read my comments too and didn't know what to make of them, because instead of dressing Velichkin's son for the game he dressed this great big guy named Strelkov, who came onto the ice and could barely skate. I asked my guys, "Who is that?" and they said, "He's a boxer. He plays in the second league most of the time, but he's a boxer." So I told the guys before the game, "There's a no-fight rule. If this guy gets on the ice, his express purpose will be to get somebody into a fight. If he wants to fight, let's make him play five or six or seven shifts, because by then we'll have two or three or four goals – and then I'll lift the ban on fighting. Perfection for him will be one shift, one fight, and he gets tossed out and one of our good players gets tossed with him." But it was a close game and he never actually got on the ice.

So we're in the semifinals now against Avangard Omsk, the team with Norm Maracle in goal. They've got an experienced team. They have a high budget. They've got lots of depth. Maracle usually turns his game up in the playoffs. They won their first series against CSKA very easily, three straight by big scores; and then they disposed of Red Army in three straight. So they've really cruised in the playoffs. They've played only six games, so it'll be a difficult series for sure. We beat them 5-0 at home and then we beat them again 5-3 about a month ago in a game when Travis had a disastrous night, giving up three bad goals, and we still won. We lost back there in September. So they're a good opponent for us because we've had good success against them.

The other semifinal will feature the second- and third-seeded teams, Ak Bars Kazan and Lokomotiv Yaroslav. It's coming together pretty much the way Velichkin predicted in mid-season. This year, through the first twelve series, there's been only one upset – and that was Lada, a ninth-seed, eliminating Dynamo, an eighth-seed. Dynamo's financial woes (and the fact that they missed so many paycheques this season) may have had something to do with that result. They probably weren't as motivated as they needed to be.

Unlike the NHL, there just don't seem to be many upsets in the Russian playoffs. The top four teams are the ones that are left, and interestingly, all four teams have Canadian goalies: Norm Maracle plays for Omsk, Steve Valiquette plays for Lokomotiv Yaroslav, and Freddie Brathwaite plays for Kazan. There are other Canadian goalies in the league, and this says a lot about our goalkeepers.

After a year of going practically injury-free, our biggest problem right now is that we've developed a serious manpower shortage. Platonov hurt his ribs in the 7-0 game; he played part of the game but couldn't continue because the rib popped out. The cartilage gave way and the rib has protruded, so we don't know how long he's going to be out, but he's out. Gusmanov came in and started in Platonov's place, but halfway through his first game he was in front of the net on a power play and got hit on the heel with a puck and broke his ankle. So he's gone too. Varlamov rode the bike today and we hope to get him back for Omsk, but I'll know more about him tomorrow. Pestunov won't be back until the series is over; if we go to the final round, he might be back. He tore ligaments in his shoulder on the second shift in the first game against Lada, so he'll be out for an extended period of time.

March 29

After practice today, our coaching staff met to discuss our line combinations in light of our injury situation. We're thinking of using The Fish again, our problem child. He's played the last two games now and hasn't looked great. He has huge amounts of skill, but he hasn't played much since the Olympics. Still, he's suddenly gone from the doghouse to the penthouse and might be playing with Kaigorodov. But you worry about him in big-game situations because he's the kind of player who doesn't compete very hard. Some nights, you'll love him because he might score, but he might also give away a couple of goals.

He's just the opposite of Malkin, who had a great series against Lada. It got so bad that Lada decided to have a guy stay with him the whole time. I had a field day with that strategy. I put Malkin at centre on two lines; I also had him playing wing on another line. I told Malkin, "Go behind the play. If their checker's on you, just circle behind our own defencemen and take him right out of the play, because then we're going up the ice four-on-four." When we'd get to the zone, Malkin would be coming from behind with lots of speed and could outskate the guy who was shadowing him – because no one can skate with Malkin when he gets going. So we'd get to the blue line four-on-four and then Malkin would get enough separation from his shadow that he'd come in late, with speed, wide open for a pass.

When Malkin got tossed out of the first game he took a lot of criticism from the press. He came back with a vengeance in the 7-0 win. Then, in the third game, we were up 4-3 and they gave us a penalty. When a team pulls its goalie, it's standard playoff procedure here that within about thirty seconds the referees give you a penalty, so it's rarely ever six-on-five. It's always six-on-four.

So we were trying to hang on and Malkin went out to the point and blocked a shot. Then he got up and, with the puck loose in the neutral zone, he took three steps and dove and poked it over the red line, out of danger, clinching the win for us. I mean, he may be getting a little cocky, but he's the real deal and boy, does he compete. You can do whatever you want to him – you can try to cover him, you can hack and whack him – but he plays. He really plays. Kaigorodov disappeared in the hard series against Lada because that's Kaigorodov. But Malkin just relished the challenge because that's the kind of hockey he likes to play.

March 30

I can sense from being around Velichkin that the pressure's off now. Not that's he relaxed or anything, but most of the expectations for this season have already been met. We won the Spengler Cup. We've fought hard in the playoffs. And now we're going into the semifinal series, with all these injuries. I don't think it takes anybody off the hook, though. I think we can beat Omsk, even with the injuries, but if the season were to end here, we'd finish third. That's the way it works over here. The teams that make the final get the gold and the silver. The bronze goes to the team with the most regular-season points of the two that get knocked out in the semifinal. Accordingly, no matter what happens now, we can't finish any lower than third and we're guaranteed to win a medal. I don't sense any complacency, but no matter what happens from here on, I think we can consider the season a success.

The more we get these injuries, the more I feel we're digging down deeper. It's been good for our team. I sense that some of the guys are on a mission; that some who weren't front and centre are now playing. They've come from the taxi squad to the lineup and I'm hoping they respond for us. Travis has been shaky. I got the sense in the last game after we made a couple of mistakes and he bailed us out, that he was getting his game back. I read his game not by his saves but by how he handles the puck – and since the Olympics, he's just like Patrick Roy, he passes it to the wrong team and has to scramble back and make a great save. He's second-guessing himself and taking too long to make a play, which causes some difficulty. If he gets it back, then we're going to be tough. From about the five-minute mark, suddenly, he looked like he was out a little higher in the crease, he looked like he had his edge back, he looked assertive – and he hasn't looked like that for a while now.

There's also good news on the home front. My son Scott's season wrapped up in Germany, so he's coming in later in the week to watch one of our games and see where we live. Then, when we travel to Omsk for the third game of the series, he and Linda will fly to Moscow for a short two-day tour before he returns to Canada. He's finished third in the league in scoring and has signed a new two-year contract in Nuremburg for next year, so he's feeling very content.

March 31

Varlamov, Pestunov, Gusmanov, and Platonov can't play, so tonight, for our opening game against Omsk, four guys who've played for us all year weren't in the lineup. On defence we'd been alternating Biryukov and Boikov as our eighth defenceman; tonight they both played. Up front, Gladskikh was in and so was Dobryishkin. It was a tight, tight game. They scored first, when Artem Chubarov connected midway through the second period. Chistov replied for us about nine minutes later and it stayed that way through the end of regulation. Time was running out in OT when one of their young players, Nikita Nikitin, scored an unbelievably flukey goal against Travis – a shot goes wide, goes off the backboards, hits our goalie, and goes into the net. It's only Nikitin's second goal of the season and came with less than two minutes to go. We lost 2-1.

We outshot them 38-20, which was pretty indicative of the scoring chances. We outplayed them, but Norm Maracle performed very well in goal. Afterwards, at the press conference, someone asked their coach, Valeri Belousov, about Maracle. He answered, "Maracle is very serious, a real pro," and indicated that when he spoke with him before the playoffs began Maracle promised he'd be on his game. He was tonight. You can beat yourself to death over lost chances or the fact that the luck just wasn't with us tonight, but it happens.

April 2

With my son Scott in attendance for good luck and Varlamov back in the lineup after recovering from a concussion, we squeezed out a 4-3 win but not without a few anxious moments along the way. We were up 3-0 just past the halfway point on goals by Yushkevich, Eduard Kudermetov, and Eriksson when we started to lose our grip on the game. They scored once before the second period ended and then twice more in the third to tie it up. Just as it looked as though we were heading to overtime again, Vorobiev scored what should have been the winning goal, except the goal light didn't go on and play continued for more than a minute. Finally the play stopped, they looked at the replay, and since the goal was clearly in they had to turn the clock back to that point. But Omsk didn't like the call, and they went crazy. Their captain, Ryabykin, threw his gloves on the ice and pushed the referee. They succeeded in intimidating the referee, so on three different occasions he went back into the penalty box and looked at the tape. It must have taken twenty-five minutes to sort this thing out. Finally, he came back for the third time and he was adamant – he pointed to centre ice and called it a goal. Even then their coach wouldn't put five players on the ice for the faceoff, but the referee didn't do a thing – no penalty for unsportsmanlike conduct; he just took it. In thirty years I've never seen anything quite like it.

That was the night that the second-ever Canadian coach in the Russian Super League came to the game. Mike Krushelnyski, who played with Edmonton, Boston, and Detroit in a career that spanned fourteen years and three Stanley Cups, and who then did some coaching on Dave Lewis's staff with the Red Wings, was appointed the new coach of Vityaz a few days ago. Mike and the Vityaz people came in to watch the second game and I thought he might come down to the locker room to say hello, but maybe because of all the controversy swirling about the result, he decided not to. Apparently, Igor Larionov, who played with him in Detroit, made the contact for him. Everybody here asked, "Who's Mike Krushelnyski?" I knew who he was as a player, but I didn't know his coaching background. I think there may be one or two North American coaches coming over. That's what the rumour mill suggests anyway. I think our good season may open some doors for other Canadians who may want to try this.

April 3

More bad news about our goalie, Travis Scott: he pulled a muscle in his hip some time ago and aggravated it again the other night. We're hoping he can play in the third game. He had to go to an acupuncturist for relief and the first time it didn't work out so well, so we found another guy yesterday and it looks as if it helped him a little bit. He's also had a problem with dizzy spells. They had to take blood tests, and our medical staff, along with everyone else, is quite concerned. It couldn't happen at a worse time. He'd been a Rock of Gibraltar for us up until now.

April 4

It's the third game of the Omsk series, and one general observation as we're getting down to crunch time: as the NHL playoffs move along, the intensity tends to go up but the artistry comes down, and that seems to be true for Russia as well. Everybody is playing it closer to the vest, and as a result the games are all really tight.

Tonight it was 1-1 until early in the third period, when we went ahead on a goal by Gladskikh. I'd told Travis before the game,

"We're having difficulties with faceoffs against this team right now, so if you don't have to freeze the puck late in the game, don't freeze it." So we get to the final minute nursing a one-goal lead and he makes a save, freezes the puck, and then looks over at me. I could see him going, "Oops." Anyway, they win the draw, Gusev shoots a puck through a crowd and it goes in, and they tie it up with exactly one minute to go in regulation.

In overtime, Vitali Yachmenev, who played for the Nashville Predators briefly but broke in as an NHL rookie on a line with Wayne Gretzky on the Los Angeles Kings, scored the winning goal. It was only his fourth goal of the season, but it was a back-breaker for us. We were playing four-on-four. We had Chistov and Vorobiev on the ice. Both the forwards got caught out at the same point. The puck was passed from that point man down to the corner area, and then it went cross-crease right away and Yachmenev was just sitting there to put it in.

In the first game we lost in overtime, at home, we'd put three pairs of two forwards together – two very offensive pairs and a third pair, Korolev and Vorobiev, very defensive. But it didn't work that well, so for this game we decided to balance it off and play an offensive player with a defensive player – and it didn't work again. To surrender a lead with sixty seconds left in regulation and then to give up a goal so early in overtime was devastating. It turned so quickly. We were all thinking, We're going to win our game on the road and no matter what happens in the fourth game, we're going back home and we'll be fine. We played a terrific game. We played so hard. We did so many things so well and then, just like that, it slipped through our fingers. Of course, your immediate thought is, How will the team bounce back?

April 5

Travis Scott went for blood tests today and the results were inconclusive. He's dizzy at times, but you have to admire his competitive nature. Days off in Omsk don't present a lot of options at this time of year because we're back in Siberia again and it's still cold. The temperature is only minus ten, but the wind makes it seem a lot colder.

April 6

Facing elimination tonight, we got off to a pretty good start in Game 4, needing a win to force a fifth game back home. Chistov opened the scoring for us on a first-period power play, but they got that one back almost right away when Chubarov scored to tie the game. They went ahead 2-1 in the first minute of the second period, and that's the way it stayed until very late in the third period when we desperately needed a goal to tie and force overtime – and we got it. Platonov missed the first two games of the series, but he came back in the last game and gave us the goal. We call it an inside two-on-one because one of their defencemen, on a three-on-two, overplayed the puck carrier, so we popped it through to the man driving to the net and suddenly we had a two-on-one – and Platonov just buried it.

In the overtime, Platonov broke in on a breakaway and couldn't score and then Chistov had a breakaway and couldn't score either. Two pretty good scorers for us, who normally bury their chances, couldn't score on their breakaways – I had a bad feeling after the second one didn't go in.

Once again the refereeing was erratic, and tonight it just killed us. Twice in the overtime we had to kill off four-on-three power plays – on cheap, questionable calls. None of them involved anybody in front of the net. None of them involved anybody going to the net. One happened in the corner. One happened up by the blue line, up by the boards. We killed the first one, but the second time we just couldn't keep it out of our net. Gusev, who scored the tying goal in Game 4 and is kind of a stay-at-home defenceman, scored this one too – to eliminate us. Gusev isn't even an offensive guy for them, he's more of a stability guy, but in consecutive games his long shots from the point have found a way to go in. If any two players hurt us in this round, it was their two defencemen – Gusev and Kirill Koltsov, a Vancouver draft choice, who's a terrific offensive player. The two of them and Chubarov were involved in all the winning goals.

The most disappointing thing was how iffy the penalty calls were. We were less than three minutes away from a shootout, and we've been so good in shootouts all season; I really thought that if we could just get there, we'd be going home to play a fifth and deciding game in the series. I didn't say anything about the refereeing afterwards because what would be the point, but our management stormed the referees' room after the game and asked them, How could they do what they did? By then it was too late. The game was over, we were done – and our extraordinary season had come to an end in the blink of an eye. The guys were really disappointed – they had truly played hard and played well. We didn't get anything to go our way in the overtime, but it wasn't for a lack of effort.

That's the solace we took out of it, that and the fact that we won the bronze medal. In the Russian Super League there's gold, silver, and bronze, just like in the Olympics. Velichkin came into the dressing room afterwards and wanted to talk to the team about how hard they played – and that was fine. But then he said to the guys – and he was very proud of this – "We've won the bronze medal; we finished third overall." Then he talked about all the records we set.

He was very happy, while everybody else was disappointed. I give him credit, though, because I know he was trying to make everybody feel better, but I don't know if the timing was exactly right.

As for Malkin, he played as hard as he could play, but I think all of us would agree that what we thought might happen, did. At the end, he just ran out of gas. He's a great kid and he played as hard as he could play, but as the Omsk series wore along, he just wasn't as effective as he'd been in the previous rounds. He didn't score a goal. He did pick up four assists in the four games. He just looked real tired after the Lada series. He played a lot for us in that series after getting tossed out of the first game for that fight with Abdulin. Against Omsk, he got some points off the power play and off a couple of faceoffs, but he wasn't as dynamic as he was at other times in the season. I wasn't surprised. He played a lot of hockey this year and he played a lot of emotional hockey – world junior, Olympic Games. At the world junior, they were in a gold-medal final and didn't win. At the Olympic Games, they beat Canada and everybody was so high afterwards, believing that Russia might win the gold – and they didn't. For Malkin, the emotional price was far greater than the physical price. He competed as hard as he could. I was absolutely proud of this young man, but he was running on fumes at the end.

The Russian papers were quite hard on him throughout the playoffs. When he got tossed out against Lada, the papers said, "He didn't get it done in the gold-medal game in Vancouver; he didn't lead his team to a medal in the Olympics." They said he was young and impetuous and had to learn to be more poised. That was the sort of thing the kid was reading, and I think the comments were unfair. For goodness' sake, he's only nineteen years old. His future is in front of him – and to expect more from him, at this stage of his career, is probably asking too much.

To add insult to injury, on our charter flight back to Magnitogorsk, we had almost made it to the city when they told us the airport was fogged in – because fog trapped by the Ural Mountains often hangs over Magnitogorsk in the spring. So we were diverted to Ufa, where we landed at twelve-thirty in the morning, climbed on a bus, and took a four-and-a-half-hour bus ride home. We arrived back in Magnitogorsk at five-thirty in the morning, which perfectly epitomized the kind of day we were having. We lost, we were eliminated, and we couldn't even get home without a four-hour detour.

April 7

No one slept much last night, or this morning, I guess would be more accurate. After a short night, we reconvened back at the rink at one o'clock in the afternoon to conduct exit interviews with the players, to discuss their summer fitness programs, and to make sure the injured guys continued to visit their doctors until they received their medical clearance.

That night they scheduled a wrap-up party at the Magnitka, one of the best restaurants in town. For someone who was still trying to come to grips with the fact that our season was over, this was the last thing I expected. There was food, there was wine, there was vodka – lots of vodka – and there was cognac. There was a live band playing; there was a dance troupe that came in to perform. They couldn't have thrown a more elaborate party if we'd won the championship. In the NHL you'd still be in mourning after losing in the playoffs, even after the year we had. We felt we came up short and, except for an overtime goal here or an overtime goal there, we'd still be playing and Omsk would be having their breakup party. Back home, unless you win the Stanley Cup, the day after the season ends usually resembles a wake. But this was a celebration – to celebrate the great season we had. The fact that we won the bronze medal was pivotal, I guess.

For me, Igor Korolev, Yushkevich, Boulin, and some of the Russians who played in North America, the celebration just didn't register. We got to the semifinals and that's pretty good and we lost a real tough series – and yeah, that's okay – but we wanted to keep playing. Some guys felt really good about what we'd accomplished, but I could tell that others really weren't into celebrating very much. My North American Russians were thinking like NHLers do. They were disappointed that they couldn't go on to the next round. It's a cultural difference, for sure. You get conditioned in North America to think that anything less than a championship – a Stanley Cup, an Olympic gold medal – is a failure, and naturally that means, for twenty-nine NHL teams per year, or eleven teams in the Olympics this year, all the ones except Sweden, the year or the tournament does become a failure.

We played fifty-one regular-season games and eleven more in the playoffs. In the playoffs we lost once in regulation to Lada and then three times in overtime to Omsk. In the end, we lost only five regulation games out of sixty-two. My rational mind tells me that's a preposterously successful season, but my heart tells me it still wasn't enough – that we had a good record against both Omsk and Kazan this season, even though they spent a ton more on payroll than we did – and that we could have won this thing. But we were all pretty close, and when that happens it doesn't take much to separate the winning team from the losing team. At the wrap-up party a lot of guys said, "We had a great regular season and we couldn't do much more, Coach. We tried to do our best, but for some reason we couldn't get a goal to go in at the right time to make a difference. We had chances in every overtime game to put it away before they did – and didn't do it." Sometimes, it's as simple as a goalie getting hot. That's playoff hockey: goalies can make a big, big difference.

And in the Omsk series, Norm Maracle made the difference. It was only ten months ago that I called him up to get a rundown on what I could expect from life in Magnitogorsk because he played there for two seasons. Norm is a very outgoing, upbeat guy. He's a little portly. He's like an old-school goalie, a Gump Worsley for this generation, which is why he never really landed a full-time NHL job. He could stop the puck all right, but his conditioning was always less than what we expect from an NHLer, even an NHL goalie, at this time. He's not slim and trim, but boy, he can play. And he had a lot at stake in this series. He didn't have a great regular season and wanted to get signed to a new contract, because Omsk and Kazan pay the best salaries in Russia. You can make more money playing for those teams than anywhere else. As well, after he played for Magnitogorsk they chose not to bring him back, which is why he ended up going to Omsk. Accordingly, he had two good reasons to play well, and he did.

I really feel good about my ability to work with the Russian players. On Friday, so many of them came over and thanked me for helping them. Denis Platonov, through the translator, said, "You took me out of the dark. For two years, my career was in darkness. I didn't know if I could be a player. But you gave me a chance and you believed in me and I never felt that way before." He added, "I'm so excited about the season I just had, and so looking forward to next season." Then Yushkevich walked up and said, "Kinger, I've never played for anyone who treated me the way you treated me. You really believed in me." The first fifteen games, I don't know if Yushkevich had a goal, yet he ended up as one of the top-scoring defencemen in the league. And his playoff stats were absolutely amazing. He may be second or third overall in playoff scoring – and he's an old warrior, with a bad leg. I said, "Well, I had a lot of confidence in you, Yesky. I appreciate guys who compete. When you couldn't score at the start of the season, you were the guy who was blocking shots. You always found a way to make a positive difference."

I had all kinds of these wonderful testaments from players and it was emotional; at times, I almost had tears in my eyes. I was thinking, Wow, I wish we'd had this party a long time ago. Varlamov, our captain, came over and said, "I just want to tell you, on behalf of all the guys, we've heard that you might not be coming back – and every guy on the roster, even those who may be going to play somewhere else, would really like you to come back."

It ended up being a terrific night. I was really pleased. Usually I leave those things early, but tonight I looked around and saw everybody having fun and socializing so well that I decided to stay. It was our last night together and they did it up in fine fashion. We had a lot of the executive from MMK there and their wives. Malkin was dancing and having a good time – the pressure was finally off. The mayor spoke, congratulating us on the bronze medal. The vice-president of MMK also spoke – Rashnikov was in Pittsburgh, trying to buy a steel mill. By the time I left, I was pretty much at peace with the result. When you get to this stage of the playoffs, there isn't much to choose from among the four remaining teams, so it sets the stage for a close series. I don't feel at all the way I did when I coached the Flames, for example, when we lost all those playoff overtime games to Vancouver and San Jose. It isn't like we left anything on the table. We emptied the tank. It's still disappointing when you're so close and you don't get a chance to play in the final, but we gave it all we had. Every game we lost, we lost in overtime, and in every game we probably had the first two or three good chances to win – and just couldn't score. Our play four-on-four was great all year, but in two of the games we made individual mistakes and it cost us. That, sadly, is the way it sometimes goes in hockey.

April 8

I have a decision to make, and soon. On Monday I'll be meeting with Velichkin to discuss whether I'm coming back or not. I've enjoyed the year, but do I want to do it again? I don't know. There was a fascination, an intrigue that was there for me this year. Next year, if I come back, I'll know the ground rules. I'll know more about the staff. I'll know more about the league. All those things will be an advantage. But I've satiated some of my curiosity, so I'm wavering. And coaching in a foreign language is a lot of hard work because you have to be so well prepared. I always have to meet with Igor Korolev beforehand and make sure the message is clear for him, because if he can't understand it, for sure the players aren't going to understand it. Still, I may come back because financially it may make too much sense. That's a factor I'll have to look at. I'm fifty-eight, after all, and somewhere down the line you have to feather your nest for the future.

I signed a two-year contract, but it was understood that I'd come over for one year and then they could evaluate whether I was the right guy or not; I'd also get a chance to review my year and make my decision.

I talked to Malkin on Friday before we left for home, just to get his thoughts. He knows he can make a lot more money in Russia, but he doesn't concern himself too much with that. First and foremost, he's a hockey player. I'll be surprised if he doesn't go to Pittsburgh; I think he wants the challenge of playing with those NHL guys. And he loved the Olympics. When I asked him what was the most impressive thing about them, he said, "Oh, the players." I was hoping he'd say something like that. He was in awe of their professionalism – that was the word he used. He said that after games they'd be stretching and riding the bike, and that he had no idea professional players were that dedicated. He's very dedicated himself, but I think he figured that being in the NHL was all about driving big cars and eating steak dinners and wearing nice clothes. Instead, he saw how these guys approached hockey as a career, and how they do so many little things every day that allow them to perform so well and so consistently. That's the knowledge he took home from the Olympics – and I was impressed that he absorbed the lesson so well.

EPILOGUE

June 1

KAZAN, WITH MY OLD FRIEND ZINETULA Bilyeletdinov behind the bench and Freddie Brathwaite in goal, won the Super League championship. Two weeks after Linda and I returned home, they swept Omsk in three straight. Omsk, I was told, had nothing left after upsetting us; they lost the first two games on the road and surrendered meekly in the final match at home. So Kazan, a team that invested millions in NHL players during the lockout in the hopes of winning a championship in the thousandth-year anniversary of the Republic of Tatarsan, had to settle for a championship in its thousand and first year. By then Linda and I had had a week of holidays in Phoenix, taken our grandchildren to Disneyland, and watched the tail end of the NHL playoffs.

As I reflect back upon this mad crazy adventure, so many of the things I worried about going over to Russia turned out to be overestimated. The translation problem sorted itself out very quickly. It wasn't much of an issue at all. By the end, I'd learned a number of Russian words and expressions and could read some signs. I knew I had to learn a little bit of the language because otherwise I'd be totally in the dark – and I couldn't stand that. So I did up a little card for myself with all the Cyrillic symbols on it, and every time I'd be riding on the bus and see a sign, I'd pull out my little cheat sheet so that I could take the sign apart phonetically. It took me a couple of months to get the hang of it and there were always a couple of symbols that gave me difficulty, but after a while I became pretty good at it. And spoken Russian can be a very difficult language to absorb, but it's amazing, after a time, how your ear improves. I didn't catch every word, but I could listen to a conversation and pick up enough as it went along to get the gist. Sometimes, when we'd be on the ice together and I could tell the other coaches were getting ready to ask me a question, I'd give them the answer before they translated it into English. That was fun. That they didn't expect. Partway through the year, I was confident enough to go out, by myself, without my translator. Even with my limited knowledge of the Cyrillic alphabet, I could figure out where I was going by reading street signs and things like that. So learning a bit of the language gave me a little more control over my day-to-day life.

When I first arrived, everybody warned me about safety issues. But once I acquired the ability to read signs and get around on my own, I relaxed. I don't think I ever worried too much about safety. Sometimes we'd get home from a road trip at four o'clock in the morning and we'd bus from the airport to the arena. Since it was only about five hundred metres away from our apartment anyway, I'd say, "Igor, I'm going to walk home." He'd say, "No, no, you can't walk." He'd be nervous about me walking home, but I had no worries at all. Who's going to be out at four a.m. on a dark winter morning in Magnitogorsk anyway?

When I first came over to Russia, I thought I knew a fair bit about their tactical game and about their preparation, but I always wondered what things were like behind the scenes. What was the chemistry of these teams? What was the dynamic behind closed doors? Were they all like Sergei Makarov who, when practice was over, would just evaporate and go his own way?

I also wondered about getting players to play certain roles. In

North America, we're always into that. You haven't got equal talent from top to bottom, so you start putting people in roles. In Russia, Malkin is a top player on the first line, but my fourth-line centre man is a pretty skilled player too. In North America, the first and second line guys are skilled but the third and fourth line guys usually aren't as skilled, so you've got to sort that out. They can't play the same way the first two lines played. So that role clarification was something we needed to work through – trying to convince some guys that we needed other things from them.

We had a player, Alexei Tertyshny, who scored fourteen or fifteen goals the year before but struggled right from the start of the season. About halfway through, I said to the coaches, "Can I approach this guy and ask him to do some other things for us? Would he accept a role change? If he's not going to score as much, let's not write the year off. Let's see if he can bring some other things to the table and maybe that will kick-start his offence." They said, "Let's try it because he's a reasonable guy." So we started talking about other aspects of his skill set. He had great speed, so we said, "We want you to be the first in on the forecheck. Get in there quickly and pressure them really hard." I showed him video clips of how effective he could be in that role. He seemed to like it. I was pleased that this guy could accept a shift in his responsibilities – to become an energy guy for us and give us something in the latter third of the season. He flushed the puck out for us; he forced them into making mistakes. He didn't get a lot more points, but he was useful. So I tried making changes like that, and sometimes they even worked.

In my days of coaching in North America, my experience was that you were always selling something. That's how Bob Johnson, the Hall of Fame coach, used to describe our profession. He'd say, "We're salesmen. That's what we do. We're always selling something to our players." Over there, I found I didn't have to sell anything. The players bought into the collective team approach. It's not a star system, even though we had our share of star players. Whenever

Malkin flexed too much, his teammates would set him straight. They'd say, "Hey, we play together." My other coaches, Viktor Korolev especially, would always find the time to talk to Malkin. He'd say, "Respect your teammates." By that he simply meant, Share the puck with them, you'll get more done.

That's an approach based largely on the collective nature of their society. They want the game to stay the same and I believe it is going to stay the same, in Russia anyway. Over the years I've come to understand that a country's cultural and social systems are reflected in their hockey cultures, so you better be aware of them. When I coached in Japan, for example, the respect given to the older players was so profound that the young players wouldn't compete hard against them for fear they'd embarrass an older player. One of the most difficult tasks I had there was trying to convince players that when they stepped on the ice they had to leave this societal culture behind. They had to accept a new revolutionary competitive hockey culture, where it was survival of the fittest, regardless of age or seniority. That was one of the hardest sells ever.

At the heart of the Russian game is a distinct Soviet hangover. The players are as rigidly controlled and supervised as they were in the Tikhonov era. It's thought that if players were allowed to think for themselves – to control their own fitness programs, for example – team discipline would be lost. The team's leaders (coaches, managers, etc.) don't trust the players to accept this responsibility on their own. The players aren't trained to think; they're trained to survive. They become adults, but are treated like children. In his book *Larionov* Igor Larionov makes that point over and over – that there's a singular lack of respect for the individual. Only the team, and its overall success, matters.

Russian coaches are well educated and seem very civilized, but they can treat a player rudely and at times with great cruelty. Time and again, I saw young players scolded between periods or on the bench to the point where I thought they'd rebel or lash out. They never did, and I often wondered why they put up with the abuse. The answer: Russia may be a democracy in theory nowadays, but their team leaders can't operate in a democratic fashion. In North America we believe that great players are born with intangibles that make them great. In Russia, coaches firmly believe that great players can be made and that training is the key. They believe that those who evolve into great players have a higher tolerance for training loads and can deal psychologically with the workload and the stress better than the average player.

I found watching the kids fascinating. I tried to pick out a couple in each age group so that I'd always have two or three benchmarks to monitor as I watched a team practice. I usually took one of the better players and one of the lesser players and observed them as they moved along from month to month. Once you see how dedicated they are and how many hours of training they put in, you realize that skill development has nothing to do with anything but a lot of hard work. It took me a while to reach that conclusion, but it finally dawned on me: yes, they do different drills and yes, they approach development a little differently, but these are largely cosmetic things. What you really see is that these kids become the skilled players they are through repetition and the immense number of hours they train. They're pushed, but after a while they don't have to be pushed very hard; they push themselves.

I suspect it's the same approach outside the hockey world as well – in gymnastics or ballet or music. When you see where they come from and how they live – most of them in grim, no-frills, Spartan apartments – you get a good understanding of the Russian athlete. These people pass a lot of tests along the way. They're pushed as athletes. They're pushed in school. They get home and they help Mom and Dad around the house. They don't have all the toys and bells and whistles that everybody in North America's got. Their lives are not easy. So when they do achieve something, you feel good for them because they've had to work hard to get there. It isn't like our system, where Mom and Dad carry your hockey bag to and from the rink and if you're a good player everybody's patting you on the back. There, if you're a good player and didn't pass the puck, they're in your face.

Generally, I gained a real appreciation for athletes in Russia and for how hard it must have been for the previous generation – for the Tretiaks and Fetisovs and Larionovs. They'd play with club teams under the same system and they also played for the national team. So when everyone else got their break, short as it was, these guys were still in the *baza* with the national team. They rarely ever got time off – maybe one month in their season.

Even now, with the season over and our older players having gone home, our younger guys received about five days off and then were back at the rink. The day before we left I went back to my office to check on a couple of things, and as I walked out the door Kulemin and Ibragimov were going out on the ice for a skate. There were about twelve or thirteen of them and they practised up until the middle of May. That's Russian hockey. The season doesn't end until the spring-training session is over. Then they get about a month or six weeks off. The last thing I did before I left was veto something that Gudzik, the strength coach, proposed. He suggested we do another camp sometime in May for anyone who didn't go home, or wasn't playing for a junior team, or wasn't at the world championships. We'd have had maybe eight players on the ice, maximum. I said *nyet* to that, and I think the rest of the coaching staff was relieved. The last thing the players needed was more ice time. They needed a chance to recover from the grind of a long season, mentally as well as physically.

As far as our tactical game went, as a North American coach, I was obviously going to do some things differently in penalty killing and in our forechecking game. I thought I'd have to push these concepts hard, but I didn't at all. It was just a matter of doing some drills in training and reviewing them on video. The players were very receptive. In my coaching I've never lost the premise of explaining why we're doing something. Don't just do the drill to do it well and then forget about it; what we want is application to the game. I found the Super League guys very good on that level; at no time did they need to be pushed to accept a new concept – or to put in the necessary work to get it down pat. That's something else I wondered at the start: was I going to be too soft? Or would I be too hard for these guys? In Germany I was too hard. Here, I found my approach matched their commitment levels nicely and they really responded to my input.

Russian society is changing and North American values are becoming ever more present, but the atmosphere in the hockey dressing room remains the same. There isn't much humour. The dressing room in North America is a sacred place. It's one of the times the guys enjoy most in the game – when the press leaves and now it's their dressing room and they can play the pranks, the shaving cream in the skates, or whatever it might be, all those things that loosen people up and make a team a team. In Russia that doesn't exist very much. And they all want personal time. They spend so many hours training – sometimes three times a day, in two ice sessions and a dryland session – that they get worn out being around each other. They're together all the time, five days out of seven. They're cloistered up. So whenever there's any free time, family time, they just want to go back to their apartments and be by themselves. They're not looking for social activity at all.

My best leaders were the North American Russians. Having been influenced by playing with North Americans, they were by far the most vocal. They also led by example. They were responsible for developing our chemistry, which, for the most part, was excellent all season. One of the real mysteries of any team sport is how chemistry develops. It's usually such an elusive, mercurial thing; it comes unexpectedly and can leave abruptly. For years, coaches and sports psychologists have analyzed, dissected, and theorized about chemistry. Many conclude that you can orchestrate its development within your team. I'd suggest that while some team-building activities can assist the process, chemistry generally evolves on a day-by-day basis. At practice, during games, in the dressing room, on the bus or plane, at team meals and meetings – these are the moments when the chemistry is percolating.

Going in, I thought Russian teams played the game with so little emotion, but maybe they were simply demonstrating controlled emotion. Since they seemed so machine-like in their play, I wondered about their passion for playing and for winning. Whether it came to them naturally, or whether they absorbed it when they played in Philadelphia and Toronto, it was players such as Yushkevich and Korolev who were primarily responsible for heightening our commitment as the season moved along and helping us overcome adversity. That's when team chemistry really can accelerate. It also grows when teammates see each other working hard in practice and working hard on conditioning. They gain respect for each other, and that respect ultimately turns into trust – trusting each other to do what it takes to win on the ice. They push each other. There are no exceptions or double standards.

The Russian players don't change until they come to North America. They recognize that there's a payoff – literally – to getting points, to being good one-on-one. And they soon learn that they're expected to be good offensively – NHL teams don't bring over many Russian checkers. So buying into the team concept was the least of my problems over there.

Off the ice, life was as much, or more, of a learning experience. Many, many times I wondered, What if I was a Russian and this was my life every day – and I wasn't turning right to go to the hockey rink, but I was going left to the steel mill? I'd never met regular Russians in my other travels to the country. Only once had I ever been in an apartment block, and that was in Moscow, to visit a lady who paints these eggs that I collect. So this year gave me a real insight into how an average Russian citizen of the twenty-first century lives. I walked up and down their stairs every day. I walked to and from work every day. I shopped in the same stores they shopped in. I bought things from the same street vendors.

The one obvious thing you realize is that it's a hard life. It's isolated. It's regimented – and the gap between the rich and the poor is overwhelming. For the select few "haves" in their society, the Velichkins and Kuprianovs, things are pretty good. They live the way we do in Canada and the United States. They own the big homes and the big cars. They have everything. They live the North American dream in Russia – but that wasn't us. We lived the other way. We had no car. We took public transportation. We revelled in the smallest little luxuries. When I'd come home to the apartment and Linda had baked bread I'd be thrilled. Even at the end, we'd go to eat at the new Dublin Irish pub and order something from the menu – a hamburger – and they'd be out. Or you'd point to a salad. They'd have seven listed on the menu and you'd say, "This one?" They'd say no. "This one?" No. Finally they'd say, "Only this one" – because they only had the vegetables to make that particular salad that day.

By the end, I'd learned how tough these people really are, especially the older ones, whose pensions have been eroded by the devaluation of the ruble. We had an old fellow living in our neighbourhood who we called the Sunflower Seed Man because he sold sunflower seeds at the corner. His wife would periodically spell him to give him a break. They have a little bowl of seeds perched on a cement ledge by the parking lot, along with a little cup and little plastic bags or newspaper so that you can put your sunflower seeds in the newspaper and eat them as you walk along. He sells them all year round. Except in the bitterly cold days in February, he'd be out there – because this is how they supplement their meagre pensions. He charges six rubles for a small cup of seeds and ten rubles for a bigger one. We'd order the big one and give him one hundred rubles; he just couldn't believe it. On our last day we gave him five hundred rubles, which works out to about seventeen dollars and to him represents about a month of selling because he doesn't sell a lot. It's a hard way to grind out a supplemental living. It makes you realize that while things are changing for the young, for the middle-aged and older people it will just be survival for life. It's not hard to understand why some of them long for the old Communist days. At least they were fed. At least they didn't go hungry.

There's a Russian proverb that roughly translates, "You are who you know." These older people don't know anyone. They have none of the connections they need to get ahead in the modern world. In that respect, not much has changed. Even in the Communist days, the corridors of power were controlled by a system of connections between friends and relatives. Many are exploiting the democratic model, and because the transition from Communism to democracy was and is so poorly regulated they've been able to bleed the system. This ability to take advantage of whatever form of government exists has been prevalent in Russian history forever. The strong take from the weak, and whereas law in a democratic country is based on precedent, law in Russia is based on exception. There's an Orwellian element at work here – laws may exist, but they don't apply equally to everyone; and at times, little effort is made to hide that fact. Life is getting better in the major metropolitan areas like Moscow and St. Petersburg, but in the rest of the country the infrastructure remains dismal and out of date. You wonder if they can modernize in time so that democracy lasts, or if at some point people will democratically vote to return to the old Communist way of life – from each according to his ability to each according to his needs. It could happen.

On our last day in Magnitogorsk, we went over and fed the dogs one final time. They looked at us with those great big eyes as we walked away. It's funny how the situation with the dogs evolved. When we got here, they were literally starving. Lady, the dog that had the puppies, wasn't going to make it. By the time we left, those dogs were so well fed. They had moved from where we'd originally found them to a compound, near a warehouse on the edge of town, where they stored food. The people who worked there sometimes threw them food as well. So they were living pretty high by the end – and strangely, on the day we left, we discovered that four more had joined the group. It was fun to mother the dogs through a cold, cold Russian winter. We complicated our lives, but it was fun.

The weather was gorgeous as we took one final stroll, but the town looked so shabby. The snow had a tendency to hide some of the mess in the winter. In the spring, it was back in all its glory – glass lying around, garbage everywhere. I thought, I'm glad I was here, I have no regrets, but I'm really looking forward to going home. The people on the team treated us so well. We didn't socialize with them much – our choice more than theirs – but if you had a concern or needed something fixed, they were there right away to address the problem. At no point did I ever regret the decision to come. Good hockey fans, good people. Every day was a new adventure.

When we left, we were fifty-fifty about whether to return or not, but against all odds we've decided to go back for a second year. In the end, we figured there's still more to learn. After spending one season in Russia, it seemed as if we were just starting to understand their mentality and culture. If we gave it one more year, we could gain an even greater understanding of what is a truly fascinating, perplexing, evolving nation.

Next year the Russian Super League will have a completely different look, thanks to new rules and regulations adopted in the off-season. The future of a number of teams is in jeopardy, including Spartak, one of Russia's oldest and most established teams, which almost dropped out for financial reasons. There'll be twenty teams altogether instead of eighteen, including Khaborosk, on Russia's eastern border just across from Japan. To get to Khaborosk from Magnitogorsk will require a ten-hour plane trip – roughly the equivalent of flying to Canada to play a game. Even with Tretiak in charge of the federation, the Super League's tendency to jump into the fire and then react to the heat still seems to be its primary modus operandi. They'll make the decision to go down a road without anticipating what problems they may encounter along the journey.

The Super League also introduced a tax on import players. Probably because there were so many that did so well this year, goalies will be taxed at the highest rate – somewhere between US$125,000 and $150,000 per player. Skaters will cost a more moderate US$25,000 per player. Travis Scott will be back, but it doesn't look as if we can afford to pay Eriksson, Yushkevich, or Korolev because of a new $11 million salary cap. How they intend to police the cap is a mystery to me, but knowing what I know of how they operate now, I'm sure the big-budget teams will find all kinds of loopholes to disguise their real payrolls. Magnitogorsk pushed for the new salary cap, and intends to abide by it too. In fact, judging from the rosters – the players we've let go compared with other teams – we might be the only ones naive enough to try to operate with a budget that's been roughly sliced in half since last year. I know this: on paper, we have the youngest team in the Super League, with five twenty-year-olds, two nineteen-year-olds, and two eighteen-year-olds projected to be on my twenty-three-man roster. We'll look like Lada did last year after their mid-season player purge.

Chances are, we're going to lose more than four regular-season games. I'm not sure if we'll contend for a championship. Those opportunities come along only once or twice in every team's evolution, and I still can't shake the feeling that this year we had our chance and it just didn't happen for us. On the other hand, working with young players is something I've always enjoyed. I saw a lot of these kids play and practise last season, so I'm looking forward to seeing how much better they can get. That's the challenge – and the blessing and the curse – of every new season. You just never know what may happen next.

AFTERWORD

My second year in Russia didn't go nearly as well as my first. I lasted eight games in total. We were 3-4-1 and coming home from a road trip against Khimik Mitishi and Omsk, two of the top teams in the league. We'd lost both games by a single goal. I was actually pretty pleased with how we'd been playing – and the direction we were going in. On the Monday morning, Velichkin asked me to come in and . . . he fired me. I couldn't believe it.

There's a saying about coaches in sport – that they're hired to be fired – but when you're in that situation you can usually see it coming: the team is in a prolonged losing streak. The effort doesn't appear to be there. The coaches and players seem to be working at cross purposes. It looks as if everyone's just waiting for the other shoe to drop. None of those things were happening, so I had no inkling, not a hint, not a clue that the end was coming. I've had more than six months to reflect upon what happened and I'm still not sure I can isolate a single reason why they did what they did. In some ways, I suspect we were a little too successful too soon.

Once again, training camp began in mid-July in Garmisch-Partenkirchen for the high-altitude training. We played all the same summer tournaments we did the year before and did very well. We won more than we lost. We won the Tampere Cup in Finland again. I wish we hadn't, but we did. In some ways, I think they thought I was deliberately underplaying our chances when I preached caution about our young team and how long it might take for it to jell. I thought we'd be good enough to make the playoffs, but that we'd likely finish seventh, eighth, or ninth, and I told them so. On the basis of training camp, they may have thought we could get into the top three or four.

But I knew differently. Kaigorodov attended our training camp, but then all of a sudden he left to go to Ottawa. I had counted on him being back. I didn't count on Malkin. Even after they had announced, with much fanfare, that he'd signed a new contract with us and would stay for one more year after all, I had my doubts. But Chistov had gone, Eriksson had gone, Yushkevich had left. At that time, Korolev wasn't back. So a lot of my warriors and leaders and top offensive guys weren't coming back, and honestly, I couldn't quite understand what our team was thinking. We even had a brand-new arena scheduled to open in January that would almost double our seating capacity.

Our team was the one that had initiated the salary cap and yet, all summer long, I kept reading on the Internet about how Kazan had signed this player and Ufa had signed those two players. I kept thinking, How can these teams, under a salary cap, be doing all this – when all we're doing is letting players go? I told Velichkin, "I don't think the salary cap is going to work because there's no possible way to police it. There's no salary disclosure. There's no party on the other side, no players' association to help you keep track of what the teams are doing. All the guys we're letting go are signing with other teams for more money. The numbers don't – and can't – add up. What's going on?" He didn't have a good answer for me, although I suspect they knew I was right and that bothered him – because as soon as I left they started to add players themselves. As soon as the first transfer window opened, changes were made. They got Kaigorodov back. They signed two more defencemen. They picked up another Czech forward. Suddenly they were doing well again –

and were ready to disregard the salary cap in the same way that every other team was disregarding the salary cap.

Another probable factor was that I didn't play Velichkin's son enough and that I pushed him hard. I really felt it was important for the organization that the other players knew the young Velichkin would have to earn his stripes. That probably played into their decision as well.

But before that ever happened, we had the soap opera of all soap operas unfold in the middle of our training camp – and Malkin was at the centre of it. When I left for home in the spring, it was a fait accompli – Malkin had done his time with us, he'd stayed a year longer than Ovechkin did; and he played his heart out for us. He was ready to go to the NHL and would leave with our blessing. Or so I thought. Then, one day around midsummer, Velichkin came in and told me the good news: Malkin was staying after all. He'd signed a contract extension, under duress, in the wee hours of the morning, with all the members of the organization putting pressure on him to stay and playing the loyalty card to the hilt. They made it clear to Malkin that he owed them something. Of course, Velichkin didn't tell it that way; I found out the details later on: in early August, in the middle of the night, with his mom and dad there, after Rashnikov had flown back from Italy to meet with him one-on-one, and feeling the weight of the world on his shoulders, Malkin finally signed the contract. The next day they asked me to come into the office at nine or ten in the morning to meet with Malkin for a little talk. Thankfully, they left the room and there was just the three of us there – Malkin and me and Igor, the translator, whom I trusted.

I said, "Malk, how do you feel about coming back?" And he answered, "I don't want to stay." So I said, "If that's the case, why did you sign the contract?" And he said, "There were so many people. I was confused. I know I owe the organization something." All those things were weighing heavily on him. He's just a young guy. I think he became overwhelmed by it all and signed. The next day he realized what he'd done and the mistake he'd made. So I said, "In this case here, don't do what your head says. Do what your heart says. You should be doing what you think is right for you. Think this thing through. The season hasn't started yet, so it's not too late."

Little did I realize how he'd take those words to heart. But a couple of weeks later, on our way to Finland, we stopped to play a game in Moscow against the new team, the Wings. I was standing in the corner of the crowded dressing room, watching all the guys and Malkin in particular, and he was absolutely in a trance. I could clearly see that he was thinking, Why am I still here, doing this? Not this again. He went out in the game and scored two goals and added an assist, but when he came off the ice there was zero joy in his eyes. Not a smile – and this guy was always smiling. I thought, This is not going the way he wants. I know his heart's not here for sure.

After the game we all went to the airport and flew to Helsinki. The plane landed. We all got off and went to the luggage area to get our bags and go to the bus, and suddenly I saw people talking and waving their arms; there was a real commotion going on. So I asked Igor, and he said, "We can't find Malkin." Right away I thought to myself, Oh my gosh, he's gone and done it. They sent Igor and Gennady back into the terminal to look for him, but Malkin had vanished. They couldn't find him. He didn't come through security to get his bags. Right around then a flight was leaving for New York, and we assumed that he'd jumped on it. Later, we found out that someone from his agency came and met him and he stayed in Helsinki for a few days in a safe house and then quietly flew over to North America after we played the Tampere Cup.

Afterwards, a lot of people wondered what, if anything, we knew about the circumstances of Malkin's flight. I didn't have any inkling of it, but I remember talking to Varlamov, our captain. He speaks enough English that he can converse with me, but he's not one of my NHL Russians. He's a real Russian hockey player. And Varly had a big smirk on his face. He said, "He's going to the NHL." All the guys knew it and not one guy was pissed off, upset, or even surprised. I think they all thought this was the right thing for Malkin – every player, to a man. I think they knew that he was pressured into a decision. There were smiles on everybody's faces, as if somebody had put something over on someone. I thought, Did they know more about this than I did? The team just didn't skip a beat.

Nor did anything that Malkin accomplished in his first NHL season surprise me. I knew he'd take the NHL by storm. He was just so consistent in our league. He wasn't the sort of guy who'd have a great night and then give you nothing for the next two games. Game-winning goals, game-winning assists – he was huge. If a game was hanging in the balance, he'd elevate his play. Some players go the other way – they can't handle the pressure of the moment. He would score some unbelievable, highlight-film type goals. I remember once when Malkin stole the puck, on a D-to-D pass, killing a penalty. He was being pursued by two checkers, and one guy tackled him. The goalie was coming out, and as he's tackled the puck rolled forward, so the goalie lunged out and Malkin dove – head first, with his stick extended – and just dug the puck out of the ice and chipped it over the goalie. Then he and the goalie collided, both sliding along the ice. The guys just said, "Wow, can you believe that?"

There was obviously a lull, an emotional sag, after Malkin left, but a month after his departure, I really thought we were starting to come together as a team. Then I was sacked – and it was the strangest firing of my life. Usually when you get fired, neither party wants to talk. There are hard feelings. It's awkward, uncomfortable. Here, though, they were all apologetic. They were saying things like, "You're so important to the team. We'll really miss you." We went to the office and went over my last expense form. I gave them a buyout number based on the NHL model, and I got paid right on time. That may have been an issue for a lot of people going over to work in Russia, but it was never a problem for me. The cheques arrived on schedule and were always good. I was impressed by how they handled that part of it.

Four days later they were driving me to the airport and pouring me tea and hugging me and saying, "If you're not working, will you come back to the rink opening in January?" Of course, I was working by then. I'd taken a job with Malmo, the last-placed team in the Swedish Elite League, with the modest goal of just trying to help them avoid demotion to the second division.

But that last day in Russia was surreal. It was unlike anything I've ever experienced before. Even now, as I try to analyze why they did, I still don't know all the answers. I guess I'll have to fall back on what turned out to be my mantra for this unlikely, unusual, unpredictable adventure: it was Russia, so you just never knew what to expect.

Andy Mettler

Dave King was coach of Canada's national hockey team for nine years, and during that time he coached the team to three Olympic Games and a silver medal at Albertville in 1992. He later coached the NHL's Calgary Flames and Columbus Blue Jackets, and became the assistant coach for the Montreal Canadiens. He was working with the top team in Finland, Helsinki IFK, before Magnitogorsk began to court him.

Globe and Mail

Eric Duhatschek was the winner of the Hockey Hall of Fame's Elmer Ferguson Memorial Award for "distinguished contributions to hockey writing" in 2001. In 2000, after twenty years of writing about the NHL and the Calgary Flames, he joined Globeandmail.com, where he writes a five-times-a-week NHL column. A frequent contributor to *Hockey Night in Canada*'s Satellite Hot Stove segment, he has covered four Winter Olympics, twenty Stanley Cup finals, every Canada Cup and World Cup since 1981, and two world championships. Most recently, he was appointed as the newest member of the Hockey Hall of Fame's annual Selection Committee.